LOOM
KNITTING
PRIMER

LOOM
KNITTING
PRIMER

ISELA PHELPS

St. Martin's Griffin
New York

A QUINTET BOOK

For information, please address St. Martin's
Press, 175 Fifth Avenue, New York, N.Y. 10010

www.stmartins.com

Library of Congress Cataloging-in-Publication
Data available upon request.

ISBN 13: 978-0-312-36661-2
ISBN 10: 0-312-36661-2

QUIN.LKP

This book was designed and produced by
Quintet Publishing Limited
6 Blundell Street
London N7 9BH

Senior Editor: Ruth Patrick
Editor: Katy Bevan
Designer: Steve West
Photographer: Paul Forrester
Photographic Art Director: Katy Bevan
Illustrator: Anthony Duke
Creative Director: Richard Dewing
Publisher: Gaynor Sermon

10 9 8 7 6 5 4 3 2 1

Manufactured in Singapore by Pica Digital
Pte. Ltd.
Printed in China by SNP Leefung Printers Ltd.

Picture Credits: Getty Images p8

Contents

Introduction

The knitting loom family can be divided it into three subdivisions: the circular looms also known as knitting looms, double-sided rake looms, and single-sided rakes.

Sit down, grab a loom and some yarn and let's begin an adventure. You can be knitting away in a few minutes.

Loom knitting is so easy; children and adults have come to embrace it as a relaxing pastime. You may recall using a wooden spool with four small nails to make long pieces of knitted cord. The miles of cord would eventually be transformed into hot pads, placemats, and coasters. Today's knitting looms are a bit different than the spool of cherished memories, but they are still as easy and fun to use.

Knitting looms come in various shapes and sizes: some are rectangular, some are round, and some are even heart shaped. The size of the knitting loom dictates the size of the knitted piece that it can make. However, you can attach panels together to make wider items. You can create almost anything with a knitting loom from knitted tubes for hats or socks, to flat panels to create scarves, belts and even sweaters.

Loom knitting is an easy craft to learn; children and adults alike can learn in a few hours. Adults who have previously struggled to needle knit can make their knitting dreams come true. Crafters, who thought their crafting days were behind them, can enjoy creating again with knitting looms.

This book is designed as a hands-on book, as well as a reference book for loom knitters. Throughout the book, you will find loom knitting techniques for both round looms and knitting boards, along with practice projects to consolidate your new skills as you learn them. Further patterns are included with fashionable designs to get you started in your new loom knitting adventure.

Loom on!

Isela Phelps

Knitting Without Needles

It is believed that before knitting needles and crochet hooks, there was knitting without needles. First, it occurred through the magic of finger knitting of the North American Indians.

Soon after finger knitting, people discovered they could knit on sticks rather than using their fingers. The sticks were short and upright in a row, not like knitting needles are used, but rather like finger knitting with sticks. It is believed that these knitting sticks were the predecessors to the Knitting Rake or Peg Knitting as we know it.

The earliest knitting rake found was found in Germany, dating back to around 1535. Early knitting rakes were made from different natural resources: wood, animal horns, and even ivory.

The oldest survivor of the knitting loom family is the cherished Knitting Spool (known also as corker, knitting nancy, and knitting noddy or French knitter), which is very closely related to the Lucet. A Lucet is a two-pronged device, traditionally made of wood.

The yarn is wound in a figure eight around the two prongs, thus creating a long and strong cord. Adding beads to the cords transformed a simple cord into jewelry.

Traditionally thought of as a children's toy, the knitting spool has four or six small prongs that are used to make thicker cords than those created on the Lucet. The cords can be sewn together to form rugs, coasters, and placemats and like the cords created on the Lucet, adding beads can add some pizzazz to a simple cord.

As you can see, knitting looms are not new to this world. They have a rich history that can trace itself back at least 400 years. Although you will be hard pressed to find an ivory knitting frame, knitting looms today can still be found in a grand array of

assorted shapes and sizes that can make your mind go around in circles. Knitting looms are currently being manufactured in wood and plastic, with the choice of wooden, plastic, or metal pegs.

Knitting looms, like knitting needles, come in different sizes. Although still being standardized in the industry, there are some recurring sizes among the knitting loom vendors. Currently, the sizes are being classified as large gauge, regular gauge, small gauge, fine gauge, and extra fine gauge. The smaller gauges are available only with metal pins to allow for a tighter stitch.

The gauges are determined generally by the distance from the center of one peg to the center of the next peg. The distances currently available can be seen in the table on page 14.

Opposite: Spool knitting used to dramatic effect by Françoise Dupre, *Knit 2 Together* at the Crafts Council, London, 2005.

Glossary

Anchor Peg
The side peg on a knitting loom. Some knitting looms have a peg or thumb tack at the base of the loom. The anchor peg can be used to anchor the yarn.

Anchor Yarn
The yarn that is wrapped around the anchor peg on the knitting loom.

Basic Bind-Off
The Basic Bind-Off method is the method used to remove items off the knitting loom.

Beginning Tail End
The beginning yarn end found before the slip knot.

Bind Off
Removing the item off the knitting loom. Knitting the very last row.

Bind Off in Pattern
Bind off the stitches as they are: knit the knit stitches, purl the purl stitches as you bind them off the knitting loom.

Block
The process of laying the knitted pieces flat on a surface, wetting them and giving them their shape.

Cast-On Row
The first row on the knitting loom.

Casting On
The process of setting up the very first row. It becomes the foundation row of your knitted item.

Chunky Braid Stitch
A variation of the single stitch. Loom must have 4 loops on each peg to start knitting the Chunky Braid stitch. Take yarn towards the inside of the knitting loom, wrap around the peg in a counterclockwise direction. Lift the bottommost 3 strands off the peg.

Double-Sided Frame
See Knitting Board.

Double-Sided Rake
See Knitting Board.

Double Stitch
A variation of the single stitch. Loom must have 2 loops on each peg to start knitting the double stitch. Take yarn towards the inside of the knitting loom, wrap around the peg in a counterclockwise direction. Lift the bottommost strand off the peg.

E-wrap
It is the method by which we wrap a peg to form the Twisted Knit Stitch.

Fashion Stitch
Used on a knitting board, the Fashion Stitch provides an open weave.

Figure 8 Stitch
Used on a knitting board. It provides an open weave, recommended for novelty yarns.

Flat Removal Method
See Basic Bind Off.

Flat Stitch
See Knit Stitch.

Frog
Removing an item off the knitting loom as a result of a mistake.

Garter Stitch
Formed by combining a row of knits and a row of purls. Perfect for items that need to lay flat.

Gather Removal Method
The method used to close the top of a hat.

Gauge
Also known as knitting tension, this is the number of stitches and rows per inch. The size of each stitch varies depending on the yarn, knitting loom gauge, and loom knitter's tension.

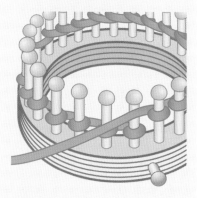

Graft
Join two edges together in an invisible way. See Kitchener Stitch.

Knit Stitch
One of the foundation stitches. The Knit Stitch is done by placing the working yarn above the loop on the peg, inserting your knitting tool from the bottom up through the loop on the peg and catching the working yarn. Pull the working yarn through the loop on the peg. Remove the loop off the peg and place the newly formed loop on the peg.

Knitting Board
A double-sided rake. It creates a double-sided fabric that has no wrong side.

Knitting Loom
A general term that is used to refer to all types of looms, that is: circular, knitting frames, single-sided rakes.

Knitting Off (KO)
Same as Knitting Over.

Knitting Over (KO)
The process of forming a stitch. To knit over, you need to lift off one (or more) of the loops on the peg and let it fall off towards the center of the knitting loom.

Loom Gauge
It refers to the measurement from peg to peg. Usually measured from center of one peg to the center of the next adjacent peg. Loom gauges range from extra fine (³⁄₁₆ ins.) to extra large gauge (¾ ins.)

Lifeline
If you have a dropped stitch, place a line of stitching, or a stitch holder in the row below to stop it running.

Purl Stitch
One of the foundation stitches. The Purl Stitch is done by placing the working yarn below the loop on the peg, insert your knitting tool from the top down through the loop on the peg, catch the working yarn. Pull the working yarn through the loop on the peg. Remove the loop off the peg and place the newly formed loop on the peg.

Reverse Stockinette
The bumpy side of a knitted fabric, formed by purling every single row.

Rib Stitch
A stitch that is formed by combining Knits and Purls.

Ribbing
See Rib Stitch.

Seaming
The process of joining two pieces of knitted fabric together.

Short-row
A technique used in shaping, it adds rows to a segment of the knitted piece. Used in loom knitting for shaping the heel and toe section.

Single-Sided Rake
A row of pegs that is used to make flat panels. A circular knitting loom can be used as a single-sided rake. A double-sided rake/knitting board can also be used as a single-sided rake by simply using only one side.

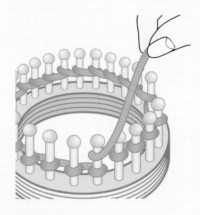

Single Stitch
The Single Stitch is done by wrapping around the peg in the e-wrap method. Loom must have one loop on each peg to start knitting the single stitch. Take yarn towards the inside of the knitting loom, wrap around the peg in a counterclockwise direction. Lift the bottommost strand off the peg.

Slip Knot
It is a knot that is placed on the first peg. It becomes the first stitch.

Slip Stitch
Slipping a stitch on a knitting loom is done by simply skipping the peg. To slip the stitch, simply skip the peg with the yarn behind the peg.

Stockinette
The smooth side of a knitted fabric. It resembles small Vs. Formed by knitting the knit stitch or twisted knit stitch every single row.

Swatch
A piece of knitted fabric that is used to determine gauge.

Tail End
The yarn that remains at the end of your knitted project.

Thread Loom
The process of casting on the very first row. See Cast On.

TINK
The word KNIT spelled backwards. It is done when you have made a mistake a few stitches back and you simply Un-knit the stitches.

Twisted Knit Stitch
See Single Stitch.

Weave in ends
When the knitted item is completed, you need to hide all the yarn tail ends. You weave the yarn tail ends into the wrong side of the item.

Working Yarn
The yarn coming from the yarn skein that is being used to knit on the knitting loom.

Meet the Family

The knitting loom family can be divided it into three subdivisions: the circular looms also known as knitting looms, double-sided rake looms, and single-sided rakes.

Circular knitting looms can be used to make a specific size tube by knitting on them in the round. Each circular knitting loom can only create a specific size of tube. The bigger the knitting loom, the bigger the tube it can create. They are formed by a continuous row of pegs that can be a circular, oblong, octagon, square, or even heart shape. The base shape of the loom does not have an impact on the look of the knitted item, as long as the loom has a continuous row of pegs.

Double-sided rake looms are also known as knitting frames, and knitting boards. Throughout this book, we will refer to these double-sided rakes as a Knitting Board. Knitting Boards have two parallel rows of pegs with a gap between them that allows the knitting to fall through. Knitting Boards are used to create double-sided items that have no wrong side. (To learn more about Knitting Boards see page 108).

The single-sided rake is a knitting loom with a single row of pegs that is not continuous. It is used to create a flat panel with a reverse and right side. Both, circular looms and knitting boards can be used as a single-sided rake to knit flat panels. When a loom is being used to knit a flat panel, it is said that they are using it as a knitting rake.

During my loom knitting journey, I have seen knitting looms being sold in different shapes, sizes, and colors. I have seen knitting looms being sold exclusively as single-sided rakes. A piece of advice if you have the choice of purchasing a round loom or a straight knitting rake, I recommend you get the round. Although they can both be used as a knitting rake, the round has the advantage of being more versatile as you can use it to create tubes.

Another advantage to knitting on a round loom is that with a straight knitting rake you will need to hold it on your

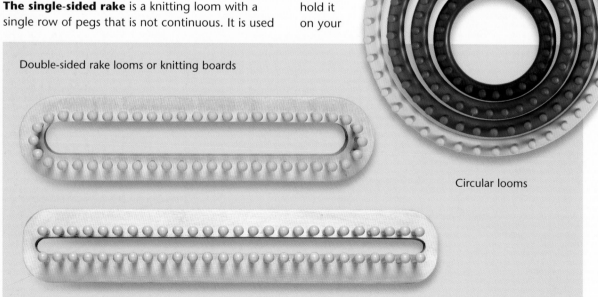

Double-sided rake looms or knitting boards

Circular looms

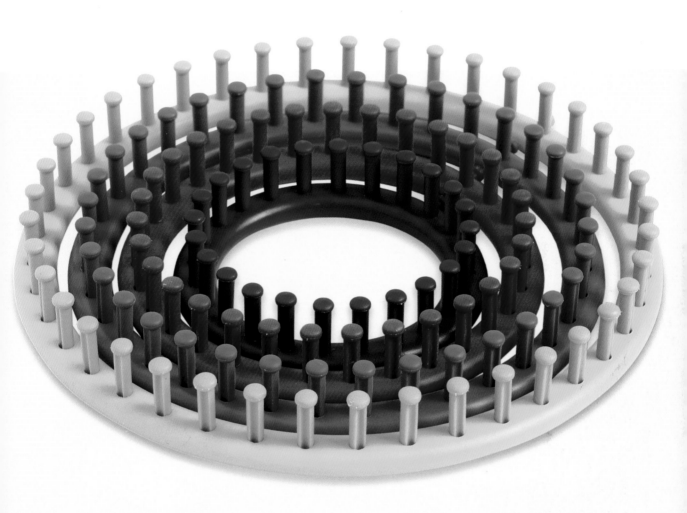

lap and look down to work, thus straining your neck muscles. Or you can hold it with one hand and wrap and knit with the other, thus putting strain on your wrists. With the round knitting looms you have the benefit of using it standing up, perpendicular on your lap, and turn it as you wrap and knit, leaving all the weight of the loom and the knitted item on your lap.

Remember, any knitting loom can be used as a knitting rake to make flat panels. Although the knitting loom may have a "designated" name, do not feel obligated to use it solely for that purpose. If the knitting loom is called a hat loom, it is only called a hat loom because it can make a tube that will fit a head. However, that same knitting loom

can be used to make panels for a baby sweater, dishcloths, panels for a blanket, and any other garment that can be made by piecing together knitted panels.

How to choose the perfect knitting loom for you? The truth is that you are the only one that can answer this question. You will have to take each one for a spin until you have found the perfect one that makes you feel comfortable.

In your journey, you will find that some knitting looms work better with different yarns. Different pegs let the yarn slide off easier, or maybe you want a little bit more resistance between the yarn and the peg so the yarn doesn't come off flying off the pegs. A little experience will help in your search.

Buying a Loom

It may seem daunting at first, as there are so many different looms available.
Don't panic; you will soon be adding to your extensive collection like a pro.

Knitting looms, like needles, can become expensive,
especially if you want to have each size available at
your disposal. Before purchasing one make a list of
the qualities that you are looking for—assess your
needs and see which loom can best fulfil them.

- Overall durability—will it break on the first or
  second use? If your dog happens to use it as a
  chew toy will it survive the game?
- Wood or plastic base—does the base need
  any upkeep?
- Gauge of the loom—will it allow you to knit with
  the yarns you use the most?
- Type of peg—is a smooth peg what you are
  looking for? Or do you want a bit of resistance?
  If you happen to step on it, can the peg/pin
  be replaced?
- Do the pegs have grooves to facilitate picking
  up the loops?
- Do the pegs have a knob at the top to prevent
  the yarn from accidentally popping off?

Remember, your knitting looms are your main tools
to create your knits; finding the right one will take
a little time and research.

Loom Gauge Table

Yarn Recommended	1 SUPER FINE	2 FINE	3 LIGHT	4 MEDIUM	5 BULKY	6 SUPER BULKY
Distance from center of pin to center of pin in inches	³⁄₁₆	¼	⅜–³⁄₇	½	⅝–¾	⅘
Loom Gauge	Extra Fine Gauge	Fine Gauge	Small Gauge	Regular Gauge	Large Gauge	Large Gauge
Manufacturers	Décor Accents	Décor Accents	Décor Accents	Knifty Knitter Long Series Décor Accents	Knifty Knitter Décor Accents	Knifty Knitter

Large Gauge Knitting Looms

- Distance from center of peg to center of peg: ¾ inch +
- **Available in:** wood & plastic, with nylon pegs, plastic, wood, and metal
- **Yarn:** Bulky weight yarns or 2 strands of medium weight yarns
- **Knits:** Bulky weight knits and knits that will be felted
- **Loom Gauge:** Approximately 1.5–2 stitches per inch
- Compared to needle knitting stitch gauge: size 13 (9 mm)

Regular Gauge Knitting Looms

- Distance from center of peg to center of peg: ½ inch
- **Available in:** wood & plastic, with nylon pegs, plastic, wood, and metal
- **Yarn:** Chunky weight yarns or 2 strands of sport weight yarn
- **Knits:** Medium weight knits

- **Gauge:** Approximately 3–3.5 stitches per inch
- Compared to needle knitting stitch gauge: size 10 (6 mm)

Small Gauge Knitting Looms

- Distance from center of peg to center of peg: ⅜ to ⅞ inch
- **Available in:** wood & plastic, with nylon pegs, plastic, wood, and metal
- **Yarn:** Worsted weight/medium weight yarn
- **Knits:** Medium and light weight knits
- **Gauge:** Approximately 3.5–4 stitches per inch
- Compared to needle knitting stitch gauge: size 7–8 (4.5–5 mm)

Fine Gauge Knitting Looms

- Distance from center of peg to center of peg: ¼ inch

- **Available in:** wood base and metal pins/pegs
- **Yarn:** Sport weight/DK weight
- **Knits:** Light weight knits
- **Gauge:** Approximately 4–5 stitches per inch
- Compared to Needle Knitting Stitch Gauge: Size 5–6 (3.75–4 mm)

Extra Fine Gauge Knitting Looms

- Distance from center of peg to center of peg: ³⁄₁₆ inch
- **Available in:** wood base and metal pins/pegs
- **Yarn:** Fingering weight/sock weight
- **Knits:** Light weight knits
- **Gauge:** Approximately 7–8 stitches per inch
- Compared to needle knitting stitch gauge: size 1–2 (2.25–2.75 mm)

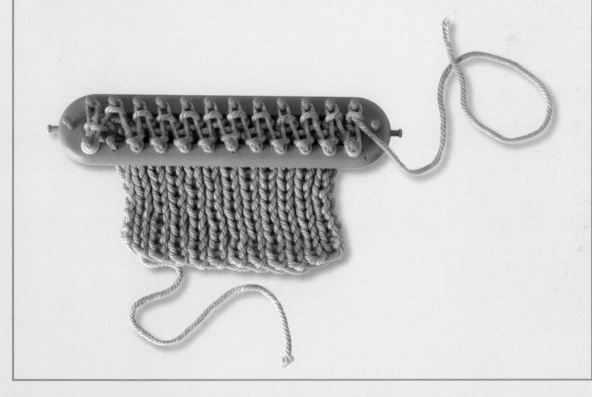

Essential Tools for your Loomy Bag

The journey is about to begin and like any journey, we need to gather our tools and gear up to make the journey easier and more enjoyable.

A Knitting Tool or Pick is the most essential gadget for the loom knitter—you can never have enough of them. Have a few of them on hand, or if you are paranoid like me, you will have a drawer full, as they are sneaky and tend to hide when you need them the most.

The purpose of the knitting tool is to facilitate knitting on the knitting looms. The tool allows you to lift the yarn up and over the peg, creating a stitch. A knitting tool is similar to a dental pick or nut pick, generally made out of metal, with a wood or plastic handle. The end is bent at an angle to allow the lifting of the stitches. Knitting tools come with different ends, some sharp for use when knitting on very small pegs and fingering weight yarns, some more blunt for use with bigger pegs and thicker yarns.

If you happen to lose all your knitting tools, you can also use a small crochet hook, nut pick, or even an orange peeler.

The yarn guide/aid is a thin plastic tube. It facilitates wrapping the yarn around the pegs and helps maintain an even tension in your wrapping. Some knitting loom vendors carry them as part of their line; if you are unable to find one, you can easily make one (see the box below).

A stitch guide allows you to determine exactly the number of stitches and rows per inch in your work. It is a flat metal or plastic piece with ruler markings on the sides. In the center there is a small L-shape window cut-out that allows you to check the rows and stitches per inch of the knitted piece. If you don't have one, you could make one out of stiff card.

To check the gauge, block the knitted piece lightly, place it on a flat surface then place the Stitch Gauge Guide on top of it. Line the bottom cut-out window opening with one row of the knitted piece. Line one of the columns of stitches to the side (see picture opposite). To determine the gauge, count the stitches per inch in the window opening. Count also the rows per inch. Make sure to count ¼ stitches and ½ stitches.

Scissors/Yarn Cutters are invaluable. Some yarns are easy to break with your hands; however, you will find that many synthetic yarns and cottons are almost impossible to break. Carrying small scissors in your knitting bag is always advisable. If traveling by airplane, I recommend obtaining a yarn/thread cutter that you can take along with you.

A Row Counter is a nifty item to have in your knitter's bag. It comes in handy… as long as you

How to make a Yarn Guide:

1 Find a Bic-style ballpoint pen with a hollow center.
2 Take out the inside ink cartridge.
3 Cut the tip off the barrel.
4 Sand any rough spots with an emery board.
5 Ready to use. Pass the starting tail of the yarn through and wrap around the pegs with the aid of your new Yarn Guide!

No pens around? No problem. Get a thick drinking straw. Cut it so you have a piece that is about 5 inches (12.5 cm) long. Thread your yarn through it and you are ready to start wrapping your yarn around the pegs.

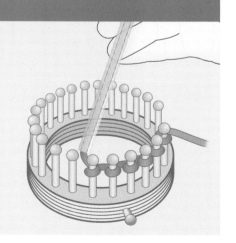

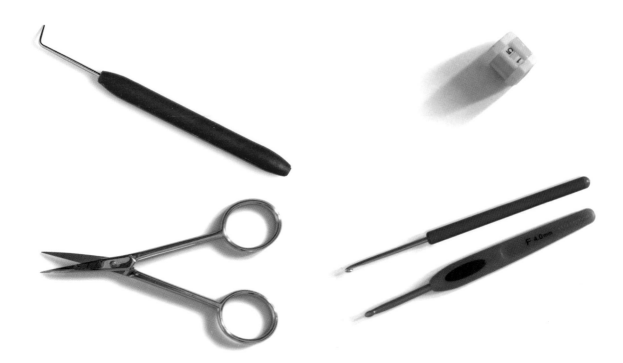

don't forget to change the setting. Row counters came in various shapes: cylindrical, square and circular. There are two types of cylindrical shaped row counter. One of them has an opening that is usually used to insert a knitting needle through; in our case it can be fitted over the knitting tool. The second one has a small ring attached to one of the sides that allows you to put it over a peg and keep it at the base of the knitting loom. The square and circular types are mechanical in that you only need to push a button to increase the numbers.

Although all of them help in keeping track of rows, you have to remember to reset them at the beginning of each row.

Crochet Hooks are very useful. Don't worry, crochet knowledge is not necessary to loom knit, unless you want to crochet an edging around your knits. Crochet hooks just come in handy when picking up a dropped stitch or when binding off a flat panel from the knitting loom. It is advisable to have the size of crochet hook called for on the yarn label, as this will make it easier to handle the yarn. In general, carrying a medium size hook in your accessories bag will suffice.

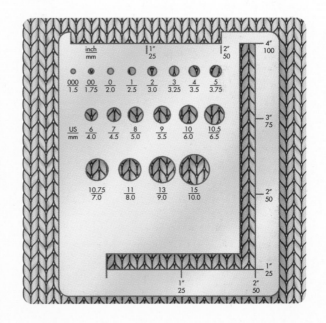

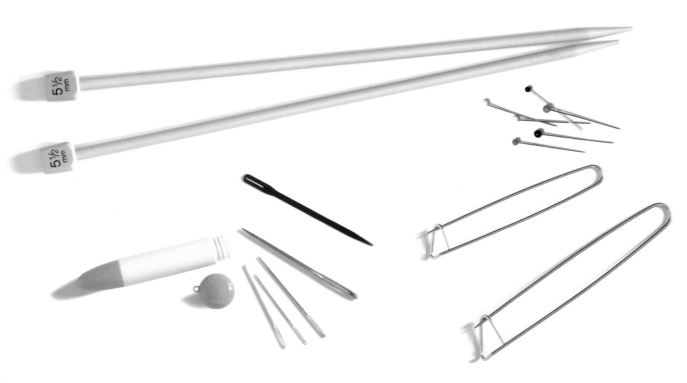

Single-Pointed Knitting Needles. Don't run, wait! You won't be using them to knit. There, you can relax! The needles are only going to be used as stitch holders for grafting the toes of socks. I would recommend obtaining a pair of size 8 (5 mm) and a pair of size 2 (2.75 mm). The size 8 can be used with the large and regular gauge looms, while the size 2 can be used with the smaller gauges.

Tapestry Needles are used for seaming the sides of a knitted garment, for gathering and closing the ends of hats, and for weaving in the ends on the knitted garment. Tapestry needles come in plastic and metal. They have a larger eye than regular sewing needles. The plastic needles are flexible and allow you to bend them. The metal needles are smoother and won't snag the knitted item. Both styles of needles have blunt ends that prevent the splitting of the yarn. As with the crochet hooks, the needles come in different sizes, and the eye opening can fit certain thickness of yarns; it is advisable to have a collection of needles that differ in the size of the eye opening.

Pins have uses everywhere in the knitting world; they can turn a curled piece of stockinette into a nice straight sleeve. They are essential tools in the finishing of knitted pieces. The straight pins with colored heads are perfect to use when seaming two sides together. Large T-pins make blocking a knitted garment a breeze. These pins can be found at any yarn shop. Do not use any other household pin as it may rust and leave rust spots on your knits.

Stitch Holders look like oversized safety pins, except they have a blunt end. They are useful for holding live stitches that will be worked on later in the project, like a neckline, or a tricky bit of shaping. They come in different sizes and it is advisable to have an array of sizes in your knitting bag. Small coil-less safety pins also come in handy when holding only a few stitches or marking the right or reverse side of the knitted item.

Stitch Markers are small rings that can be used to mark the pegs where special stitches or other special treatment needs to be done on the knitted item. Usually, the stitch markers are used on needles, however, since they are small rings, they fit perfectly over the pegs on a knitting loom and they sit at the base of the loom to remind the loomer that the peg has a stitch that requires special treatment.

Split ring stitch markers are very helpful in marking a stitch itself rather than the peg. The open split rings are removable by simply opening the ring and sliding it off the peg. They come in various shapes, sizes and colors. Having a variety of different colors is recommended.

Measuring Tape or Ruler is a loom knitter's best friend; no knitting bag should be without at least one. When choosing a good measuring tape, choose material that won't distort easily. Discard any measuring tape at the first sign of wear, even if it's your favorite. A distorted measuring tape can mean disaster to your knitted garment as it won't measure accurately. A small plastic ruler is also advisable to have on hand.

Cable Needles come in different shapes and sizes. They are available in plastic and metal. Usually, one package contains three different sizes; choose the size that best works with the yarn in the project.

Until very recently, loom knitters were not able to create cables on a knitting loom, the non-elasticity of the stitches as set on the knitting loom making it difficult. However, this has changed. Now, we are able to create cables and thus we have added the use of cable needles to our extensive gadget repertoire!

Calculator. Yep, you read it right, we will still be doing math. I know you thought math was long gone with school, but math has come to haunt you again; it wants to be your best friend. No worries though; you can cheat this time and use a calculator. A calculator comes very handy when calculating gauge or even adding a few pegs to the count in the pattern.

Other noteworthy gear for the journey

Post-It Notes
Stickies are a great way to mark the row on the paper pattern you are knitting. After knitting each row, move the Post-It down the page.

There are two schools of thought about Post-Its:

1 Cover the previous knitted row and expose the rows to come.
2 Cover the future rows and only expose the rows worked on.

It is up to you to decide which method works best for you.

Notebook
A place to jot down ideas about the patterns, comments about yarns, and other loomy gems.

Ball Winder
This little gadget allows you to wind your yarn into an easy to use center pull ball. Two styles are available, manual and electric, but you can always make balls the old-fashioned way with your hands.

Yarn Swift
A yarn swift is usually used in conjunction with the ball winder. It resembles the inside of an umbrella. It holds a hank of yarn and it unwinds it. When used along with the ball winder, the yarn swift unwinds the hank of yarn and the ball winder winds it into a ball. If you don't have one of these, persuade a passer-by to sit still with their arms outstretched while you wind your ball, or failing that, use the back of a chair.

Fingernail File/Emery Board
Is your yarn catching on the pegs? Some knitting looms have small burs on the pegs that may snag the yarn. Use the emery board to sand down the small burs and you have smooth looming ahead!

Knitting Bag
You would need a bag that is big enough to hold your project and your knitting loom. Sturdy enough to carry the weight of the knitting loom. Comfortable handle to hold or carry around. It should have a wide opening to take out and put in all your loom knitting essentials. It should have pockets, lots of pockets to put in all the yummy gadgets and notions and even a small snack for the reward moments. If possible, it should be waterproof so if it happens to rain, your knitting is safe. Closures should be either zippers or buttons; say no to Velcro—this will snag your yarn and can even destroy your knitted item if caught.

Yarn 101: A Quick Refresher on Yarn

One of the perks of any fiber art is the luxurious yarn "needed" for the projects. The market is saturated with luscious, soft, sparkly, warm yarns, varying in color, texture, and content.

Consider this a crash course on yarn. Before going all out and purchasing 10 skeins of that pretty yarn you fell in love with, let's take a small trip to the yarn shop and get personal with the yarns.

Feel them close to your skin; the neck or the inside of your forearm are good places to see how your skin reacts to its fiber properties. Check the color in different lighting, move around the yarn shop to see the effect that different lighting has on the yarn. If possible, ask if you can see it outside under real light. Pull at it to see its elasticity; some yarns have more elasticity than others and this can affect the overall look of the project.

Check the yarn label for important fiber-related information. The label band contains essential information, such as fiber content, color, dye lot (if any), washing instructions, and yardage. Keep the yarn labels of any project until you have completed the project. Recently, a friend of mine moved to a different state, at the time she was knitting a beautiful Fair Isle scarf and she ran out of one of the colors. Fortunately, she had saved the label and was able to match the exact dye lot at a different yarn shop in her new location. Moral of the story: keep your yarn labels.

Label Close-up

1 Brand Name
2 Yarn name
3 Fiber Company

4 Yarn Weight
5 Yardage
6 Fiber content

7 Care Instructions
8 Gauge Indicator
   (Needle and Crochet related)

1

ROWAN

2

handknit cotton

100% COTTON 100% BAUMWOLLE 100% COTON

6

3 Rowan Yarns
   Holmfirth
   England
   Z048000

4 50g

In accordance with
B.S. 984

5 Approx length 85m
   (93 yds)
   www.knitrowan.com

7 [40] Machine wash

Warm iron

Do not bleach

(A) Dry cleanable in all solvents

Do not tumble dry. Dry flat out of direct sunlight

8 19–20 sts
   10cm/4in
   28 rows
   10cm/4in

   8-7 UK   4-4½ mm
   6-7 US

CARE INSTRUCTIONS
Dry clean or hand wash in soapflakes; do not soak; cool rinse; do not wring; short spin; do not leave wet; reshape and dry flap away from direct sunlight; use damp pressing cloth.

Chemisch reinigen oder handwäsche mit geeignetem Waschmittel; nicht einweichen; kühl und gründlich ausspülen; nicht auswringen; kurz anschleudern; nicht nass liegenlassen; in form ziehen und flach liegend trocknen vor direkter Sonnen und hitzeeinwirkung schützen; mit feuchtem Tuch dämpfen.

Nettoyage à sec ou lavage à main avec del paillettes de savon; ne pas lasser tremper; rinçage froid; ne pas tordre; essorage court; ne pas laisser mouillé; redonner la forme et laisser sècher à plat à l'abri du soleil; repasser à vapeur.

Yarns come wound in different shapes: cones, skein, hanks, and balls. A cone has a cardboard center that has yarn wound around it. Its starting tail is on the outside of the cone. A ball is ready to use and, usually, has a starting tail in the center core. Reach your hand in the center, and pull out the center. If lucky, you will find the starting tail right away. Once you start loom knitting, do not stop until you have finished knitting all the yarn you took out from the center, or make sure to wind it loosely around the outside of the ball. A hank is a loosely wound coil of yarn, held together by a string at two sides of the coil. A skein is the hank twisted into a managable shape, and you will need to wind it into a ball.

Yarns are divided into two groups: natural fibers, and synthetics. Under natural yarns, there are two subdivisions: those that are protein based and cellulose based.

Protein-based fibers are the most well known and include wool, angora, cashmere, mohair and alpaca. Protein fibers such as wool are popular among loom knitters for their warm, elastic, and durable characteristics. Wool is known as a good all-year-round fiber.

Cotton is the most widely known vegetable/cellulose fiber. Known for its cooling properties, cotton is often used for summer garments as it absorbs moisture and dries quickly, although it does not have the elasticity of wool. Another natural fiber, silk is known for its smoothness and softness. To provide elasticity or warmth, yarn manufacturers often mix these natural yarns with other fibers to benefit from the properties they lack.

Synthetics have opened the door to a fun world of novelty yarns, think funky, sparkly, nubby textured yarns. Synthetic yarns have the great advantage of being machine washable, making them a great choice for children's loom knits. However, synthetics are hot and have little or no absorbing properties, leaving the wearer feeling like they just came out of a steam room session. Manufacturers have combined synthetics with other fibers to achieve certain qualities that other fibers may lack.

Yarn Weights

Yarns come in different thickness, known as weights. The thicker the yarn, the bigger the stitches made. Yarn weights range from fine to bulky weight. The finer the yarn, the closer the pegs need to be on the knitting loom.

The Table below gives a standard reference guide for yarn and the use of it on knitting looms. So many yarns, so little time! Choosing the right yarn for the project can be a little bit daunting when starting on the journey.

Variegated color yarns: work best with simple stockinette or other simple stitch patterns that will allow the beauty of the colors to show. Textured stitches will be hard to see through the color changes.

Solid color yarns: Recommended for cables or any other stitch patterns. Cables show better with light color yarns.

Novelty yarns: Think simple stockinette or garter stitch sto show off the special characteristics of the yarn; anything more complex won't show. Once you have chosen the yarn for your project, knit up a small swatch and wash it a couple of times. Check for the following: colorfastness, pilling, drape, shrinkage, and most importantly does it show the stitch pattern as you imagined it?

Yarn Weight Symbol	1 SUPER FINE	2 FINE	3 LIGHT	4 MEDIUM	5 BULKY	6 SUPER BULKY
Types of Yarn	Sock, Fingering, Baby Weight	Sports, Baby	DK Light, Worted	Worsted, Aran	Chunky	Bulky
Knit Gauge in Stockinette Stitch per inch	7–8	5–6	4–5	3–4	2–3	1.5–2
Recommended Knitting loom Gauge	Extra Fine Gauge	Fine Gauge	Small Gauge	Regular Gauge	Regular/ Large Gauge	Large Gauge

PART I
Round Loom Knitting

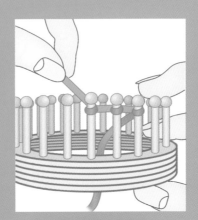

Building Blocks

Let's take our knitting loom for a little test ride. If this is your first time loom knitting, grab a skein of yarn, preferably a plain color with wool content.

Casting On

The foundation row for our loom knits is called the cast-on row. There are various cast-on methods, but we will only address the most basic one in this section. Every cast-on method starts with a first stitch known as a slip knot. Why a slip knot you may ask? A slip knot allows you to make the loop bigger or smaller by pulling on the loop. It can also untie fairly easily.

Slip Knot

1

Leaving a 5-inch (12.5 cm) beginning tail form a circle with the working yarn.

2

Fold the circle over the working yarn that is coming from the ball.

3

Reach through the circle, and grab the yarn coming from the skein.

4

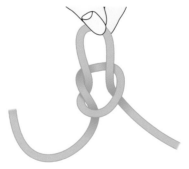

Pull the working yarn through the circle, while also pulling gently on the short end of the yarn tail end, thus tightening the noose on the knot. Slip knot completed.

After our slip knot, we are going to place our foundation row on the knitting loom. We will cover in this section the basic e-wrap on page 28.

Using the Loom

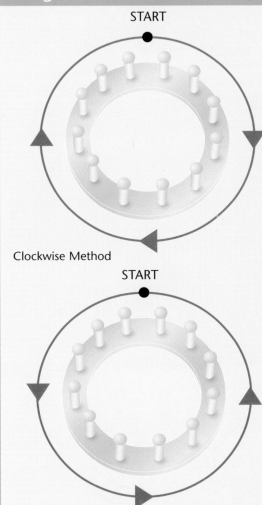

Clockwise Method

Counterclockwise Method

In loom knitting there are two schools of thought. In needle knitting, you have the Continental and English methods—in loom knitting we have the Clockwise and Counterclockwise methods.

In the Clockwise school of thought, you will find yourself working around your knitting loom in a clockwise direction. Begin knitting on the left side of the starting peg.

In the Counterclockwise school of thought, you will find yourself working around the knitting loom in a counterclockwise direction. You will begin knitting on the peg to the right of your starting peg.

Both of the methods achieve the same goal. Choose the one that feels most comfortable to you. When working on the knitting loom, it doesn't matter which way you hold the knitting loom, with pegs facing you, or opposite you, or with the loom upside down. The knitting still looks the same.

A note of warning: when reading patterns, find out in which direction the pattern is worked. If you read the pattern in the wrong direction, you will end up with a mirror image of the design. The designs in this book are worked in a clockwise direction around the knitting loom.

Loom Anatomy

There are some basic parts to the loom that you will become increasingly familiar with. This is a circular loom, but the elements are the same whether it is rake, board or round.

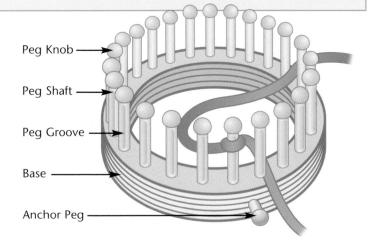

Peg Knob

Peg Shaft

Peg Groove

Base

Anchor Peg

The E-Wrap Cast On (CO)

This cast on is called the e-wrap because if you look at it from an aerial view it resembles a cursive e. It is the easiest method to learn.

Use the E-Wrap Cast On method when the first row needs to be picked up for a brim or seam or the cast-on row needs to be extremely flexible.

1

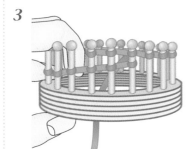

Place a stitch marker on any of the pegs on the knitting loom. The peg with the stitch marker will be your starting peg. Make a slip knot, and place it on the peg with the stitch marker.

2

Hold the loom in front of you with the working yarn in your left hand, work around the knitting loom in a clockwise direction thus: * Pull the working yarn towards the inside of the loom, wrap around the peg directly to the left, in a counterclockwise direction around the peg. * Repeat from * to * with each of the pegs. Continue wrapping each peg in a counterclockwise direction,

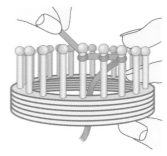

until you complete one round (each peg should have 1 loop).
Notice how the yarn crosses over itself on the inside of the knitting loom.

3

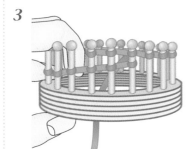

Wrap each peg a second time in the same method. Each peg should have 2 loops on it. Hold the working yarn in place so the wraps do not unravel.

4

With knitting tool/pick, insert the tip of the tool into the bottommost loop on the last peg wrapped. Lift the loop up and off the peg and allow the loop to fall towards the inside of the knitting loom. The process of lifting the loops off the pegs is known as knitting over, abbreviated as KO.
Go to the peg directly to the left and repeat Step 4, knitting over. Repeat all around the

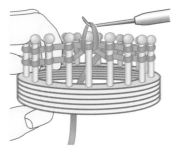

loom until each peg has only one wrap.
Steps 1–4 constitute the casting on set-up. The knitting loom is now ready.

Using the anchor peg

Some loom knitters prefer to use the anchor peg on their knitting loom to anchor their slip knot. This is a small peg that appears at the side of the loom. If there isn't one you can use a thumbtack to secure the slip knot. To use the anchor peg when casting on, make a slip knot leaving a 5-inch (12.5 cm) tail. Place the slip knot on the anchor peg on the side of your knitting loom. Perform steps 2–5 as before then remove the slip knot from the anchor peg.

First Stitches

Your foundation row is set up. Now we need to learn a few basic stitches to begin knitting on our loom. Luckily the E-wrap method we used for the cast-on can also be used to create stitches on the knitting loom.

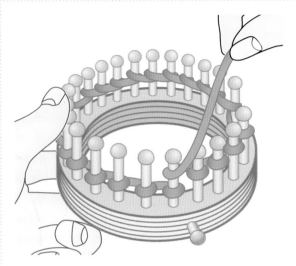 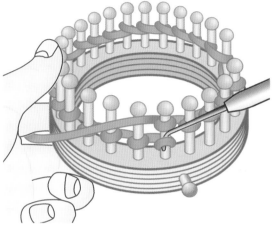

Single Stitch (ss)

To create the single stitch, just e-wrap around the peg, and 'knit over' by lifting the bottom loop up and off the peg.

The single stitch creates what is known in the knitting world as a twisted knit stitch.

Wrapping the entire loom and then knitting over may be quicker, but can create a ladder effect between the first and last peg knitted. In addition, since you are knitting in the round, if you wrap all the pegs then knit them over, your item will have a tendency to twist and you will see your vertical lines of stitches spiral around the item. Instead, try e-wrapping and knitting over one peg at time.

WRAPPING THE LOOM

Although, it is easier to wrap the entire loom two times with the e-wrap method, then lift the bottom loop on all the pegs. I would advise you to do otherwise.

Bonuses in knitting one peg at a time:
1. Will help eliminate the laddering effect between the first and last peg.
2. Help in lessening the spiral effect of the stitches around the item.
3. Less chance of the dreaded "boing" effect!
4. The stitches won't get too tight.

GLOSSARY

Boing Effect By knitting over on the last peg wrapped first, you are securing the stitches on the knitting loom to prevent them from unraveling. This sudden unraveling is known as the "Boing Effect!"

First Stitches cont.

The Double Stitch (ds)

This is also known as the one-over-two. The knitting loom needs to be prepped with three loops on each peg and the bottommost loop on the peg is lifted over and off the peg. This produces a tighter stitch than the single stitch. It also resembles the twisted knit stitch.

1

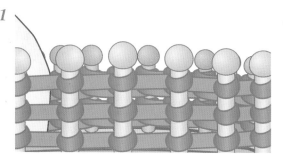

Cast on your knitting loom. E-wrap all around the knitting loom two more times. Each peg has three loops on each peg.

2

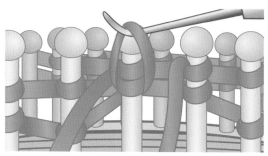

Knit over by picking the bottommost strand off the peg (two loops remain). Repeat this all around the loom until you reach the last peg.

The Half Stitch (hs)

The Half Stitch thus named as you have to e-wrap around the loom four times, then, knit over two over two. It produces a thicker stitch than the double stitch. As the single stitch, and the double stitch, the knitting will resemble the twisted knit stitch. If you are knitting with a thin yarn on a large gauge knitting loom, you may want to use the half stitch.

1

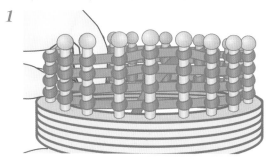

Cast on your knitting loom. E-wrap all around the knitting loom three more times. Each peg has four loops.

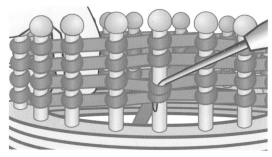

Knit over by lifting the lower two strands off the peg. Repeat all around the knitting loom. Two loops remain on each of the pegs.

Chunky Braid Stitch (cbs)

This stitch resembles a knitted braid. It is also known as the three-over-one stitch, or braid stitch. It produces a thick, non-stretchy fabric with a very tight stitch. If you are knitting with a thin yarn, you may want to try this stitch throughout your project to get a firm tension.

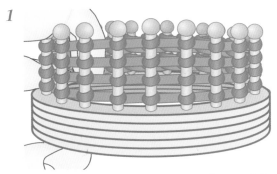

1

Cast on your knitting loom. E-wrap all around the knitting loom three more times. Each peg should now have four loops.

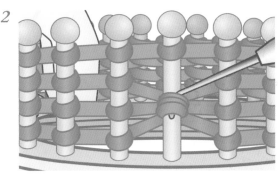

2

Knit over by lifting the bottommost three loops off the peg. Repeat the knitting over process all round the loom. One loop remains on each peg.

The above stitches are variations of stitches you can accomplish with the e-wrap method. They all produce a twisted, stockinette-stitch fabric.

Many of the variations of the e-wrap require you to wrap your entire loom first then knit over. A tightness problem arises when knitting in this form. Although you may not notice it right away, if you wrap the yarn too tight around the pegs, your future rows in the piece will become very tight, making it almost impossible to knit over.

If the yarn is wrapped too tight, try this:
- Use a yarn guide to wrap your yarn around the pegs. The yarn guide will help maintain a loose and even tension all around the loom.
- Before e-wrapping all around the loom, pull sufficient yarn from the ball to e-wrap one entire row. Having the yarn loosely next to you will help in maintaining a loose tension on your wrapping.

- When knitting over, try pulling the loop away from the peg first, then lifting it over the peg.

If the loops become too loose, try this:
- Use a yarn guide to wrap the yarn around the pegs. The yarn guide will help in keeping an even tension around the loom.
- When knitting over, clear the loop just enough to go over the ball on the peg.

Finishing

Now that we know some stitches, let's cover some basic removals.

Removing an item off the knitting loom is known as binding off, or casting off.

Gather Bind-Off

The gather removal method allows you to finish a tube into a gathered end, perfect for finishing hats. Knit the tube until you have reached the desired length. If you are using any of the e-wrap stitch variations above, knit over until 1 loop is left on each peg.

1

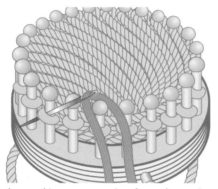

Cut the working yarn coming from the project, leave a 5-inch (12.5 cm) tail. Or if necessary, cut another piece of yarn that is at least 2 times the circumference of the knitting loom. Thread the yarn through a tapestry needle.

2

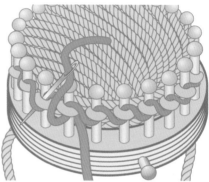

Go to the first peg, pass the needle and yarn through the loop on the peg, leaving a 5-inch (12.5 cm) beginning tail. Go to the second peg, and pass the needle and yarn through the loop on the peg. Continue around the loom. Once you have reached the last peg. Pass the needle and thread through the first stitch one more time.

3

Remove the loops off the pegs. Gently pull on the beginning and end tails of the gathering yarn. Continue pulling on the tail ends until the top of the item has been cinched closed. Poke your tapestry needle through the small hole at the center at the top of the hat. If the hole is too big, use the tapestry needle to sew the hole closed.

4

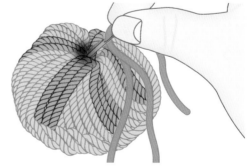

Grab the yarn tail end coming from the knitting of the hat. Tie the three strands (the two ends from the gathering yarn and the one from the knitting of the hat) together. Make a square knot and weave in the ends (see page 34).

Basic Bind-Off (BO)

It creates a firm, crochet-like edge. It is a good overall bind-off method for flat panels.

1

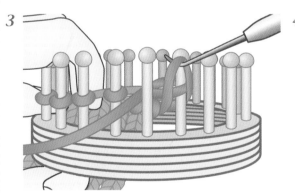

Knit two stitches (pegs 1 and 2).

2

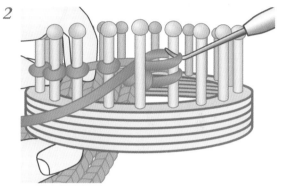

Move the loop from the second peg over to the first peg. Knit over.

3

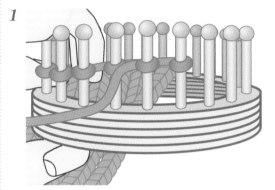

Move the loop on the first peg over to the peg just emptied.

4

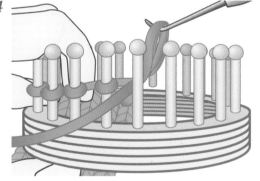

Knit the next peg. Repeat steps 2–4 until you have bound off the required number of stitches. A stitch will remain on the last peg. Cut the working yarn leaving a 5-inch (12.5 cm) tail. E-wrap the peg and knit over—pull the tail end through the stitch.

Finishing cont.

Yarn Over Bind Off

The yarn over bind-off provides a stretchy border, perfect for items that require a flexible opening like magic scarves, ruffles, leggings, or the neckline of children's sweaters.

1

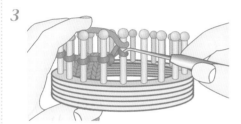

Knit the first stitch (Peg 1).

2

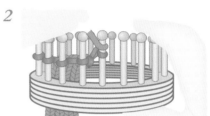

Wrap the peg in a clockwise direction.

3

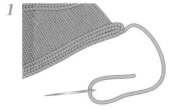

Knit over and knit the next stitch (Peg 2).

4

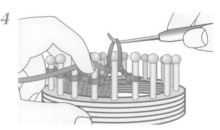

Move the loop from the second peg to the first. Knit over. Repeat 2–4. When one stitch remains, cut the yarn leaving a tail. E-wrap the peg, knit over, and pull the tail end through.

Weaving in the Tail Ends

You have finished your first project, it is almost ready to be worn, but you still need to hide those unsightly tail ends from your yarn. What to do? It is fairly simple all you need is a large tapestry needle. Work carefully on the wrong side of the item and your stitches should be invisible.

1

Locate the yarn tail end and thread it through the large eye of a tapestry needle

2

Working on the wrong side of the item weave the yarn tail end by inserting the needle through the "bump" of each knit stitch. Go up and down one row for about an inch in each direction.

Steps 1–2 should create a Z with the tail end. Cut the remainder of the yarn as close to the knitted item as possible. Repeat this process with each yarn tail end you have in your knitted item.

Brim It

Brims/cuffs are not only for hats: get creative and place a small cuff at the top of your slippers, socks, or you can even make a small cuff on the beginning edge of a sweater. Creating a cuff or brim on your knitted hats can provide you with a warmer item to wear during the chilliest months. All you need do is knit for a few inches, then place the cast-on edge back on the knitting loom. Calculate how broad you would like your cuff to be, usually about 2–3 inches (5–7.5 cm), see the chart below.

1

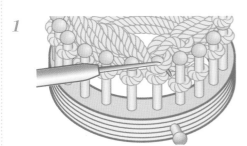

2

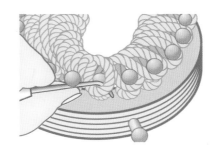

Reach inside the knitting loom, and find the beginning yarn tail end. Align the beginning yarn tail end with the first peg on the knitting loom. Next to the beginning tail end, locate the very first cast on stitch. Place the stitch on the corresponding peg. Repeat this step with the remaining stitches. Each peg should have two loops on it.

Knit over by lifting the bottom loop off the peg. After all the stitches have been knitted over, the loom should only have one loop on each peg. Continue knitting the hat in your pattern stitch.

Popular Cuff/Brim Lengths				
Cuff Length	3 ins. (7.5 cm)	2.5 ins. (6.5 cm)	2 ins. (5 cm)	1 ins. (2.5 cm)
Knit	6 ins. (15 cm)	5 ins. (12.5 cm)	4 ins. (10 cm)	2 ins. (5 cm)

TIP

You can hide the yarn tail end by sandwiching it in within the cuff. When you bring up the cast-on edge for a cuff, simply place it inside the fold.

Let's Talk Gauge

Let's take a small break and look at some numbers. Don't be scared and run away, but do feel free to reach for a little chocolate to calm your nerves. It's not algebra, honest.

When following a pattern, matching the gauge is imperative, unless fit is not a factor. For this reason alone, it is recommended to **always knit a swatch** before embarking with any project—especially if the project needs to fit a certain someone.

Let's make a swatch

To loom knit a swatch, cast on the number of stitches as called for in the gauge section of the pattern plus 10 more. If the gauge for the pattern states 4 stitches over 2 inches, then cast on 14 stitches. Loom knit the swatch on the stitch pattern called for in the pattern until it reaches about 6 inches in length, then bind off.

Measure for gauge, count all stitches; ¼ stitches and ½ stitches count! Measure in a few different places to make sure that the gauge is consistent.

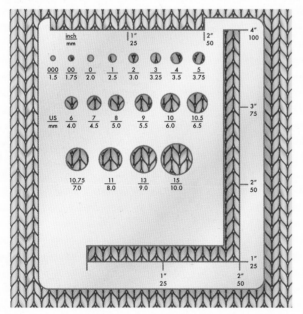

Got Gauge
You can go forth and start loom knitting! Count yourself lucky!

More stitches per inch than called for in the pattern. What does this mean? It means that if you go forth and knit with this yarn and knitting loom the item may be too small.
Fixer-uppers:
• Try with a thicker yarn.
• Try with a larger gauge knitting loom.

Fewer stitches per inch than called for in the pattern. What does this mean? It means that if you are stoic enough to continue, you will end up with an item that may be big enough to fit Goliath!
Fixer-uppers:
• Try with a thinner yarn.
• Try a smaller gauge knitting loom.

Remember that Stitch Gauge Guide we talked about in the tools section. Well, it is time to take it out for a spin (see page 17). If you don't have one, you can also use a measuring tape.

Knit a small swatch to try out the stitches. Set it on a flat surface. Set your stitch guide in the center of your swatch. Align your stitch guide so there is a row aligned to the horizontal part of the L window.

Count the number of stitches along the horizontal side of the L cut-out window. Write the number down. Now, count the rows along the vertical side of the L cut-out window. Write down the number. The numbers that you come up with are your gauge for that loom, using the type of yarn in the project, and the stitch used in the project. In this diagram, for example, there are 10 stitches across and 19 rows.

Gauge is dependent upon 4 factors:
• Yarn
• Gauge of the knitting loom
• Type of stitch
• Your personal wrapping tension

The three first elements will have the most impact upon gauge. If any of these three elements change, the gauge will change.

Playing with Numbers

If your heart is still set on a specific yarn but you still don't get gauge, don't despair, you can still continue forth. Bring out the calculator and do some math and calculate the number of stitches and rows you will need to create the same item.

Let's assume you want to knit a square that is 20 x 20 ins (51 x 51 cm). The gauge given in the pattern is 6 stitches and 8 rows in 2 inches (5 cm).

To create the square with the gauge above you will need to cast on 60 stitches and knit for 80 rows. But, your swatch tells you that you've got a gauge of 4 stitches and 6 rows in 2 inches.

To create the square of 20 x 20 ins (51 x 51 cm) you will need to make the following changes: Cast on 40 pegs and knit 60 rows.

I know it is a bit frustrating knitting swatches but it is worth taking the time to knit a small swatch. Don't look at your swatches as lost time or yarn. You can always make something with your swatches. Make small bags by knitting a rectangle swatch, fold the rectangle in half. Seam the sides of the rectangle with the mattress stitch seam. Knit a long cord (see I-cord page 51) and attach it to the bag and ta-da! Your swatch became a little bag.

Below: Each stitch affects the tension differently. For instance, the Single Stitch here has slightly lopsided Vs and will create a different gauge to any other you might choose.

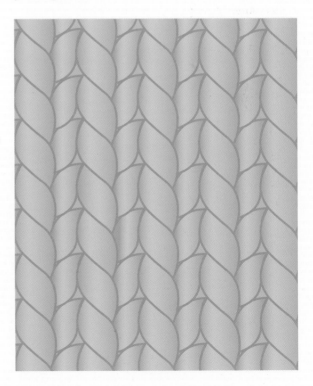

Practice Project

Simple Hat

Let's kick things off with a basic hat pattern, using what we have learned so far.

You will need

Yarn

50 yds (46 m) of bulky weight yarn [We used Rowan Big Wool in Lucky 020, 100% wool. One 100 g ball has approx 87 yds (80 m) of yarn so ½ ball should be enough depending on your tension]

Knitting Loom

Large gauge hat looms; Round Yellow Knifty Knitter for Adult, Round Green Knifty Knitter for Child size

Tools

Knitting tool
Tapestry needle

Size

Children, teens and heads up to 20 ins. (51 cm) circumference

Gauge

4 stitches and 7 rows to 2 inches (5 cm) over pattern stitch

TIP

If you don't have any bulky weight yarn, use 2 strands of worsted weight/medium weight yarn and treat it as one strand of bulky weight yarn, then check your gauge.

Pattern notes

Knit in the round using single stitch (ss).

Hat Brim

Cast on with the E-wrap Cast On method.
Knit 1 row of chunky braid stitch.

Hat Body

Knit in single stitch until item measures 7 inches (18 cm) from cast-on edge.

Crown of Hat

Decrease for the crown as follows: Move every third stitch over one space to the right. 24 stitches rem with 2 loops on each peg. 12 pegs empty. In single stitch, knit over 2 over 1 on all the pegs.

Move every third stitch over one space to the right. 12 sts rem, 24 pegs empty.
Bind off using the gather removal method (see page 32). Weave in all yarn tail ends.

Now that was easy! Your first loom-knitted item is done!

More Cast Ons

In this section, we will look into more ways of casting on (CO). Each cast on method has recommended applications. The Cable and Chain cast on methods, are the most useful.

Cable Cast On

This creates a neat, non-loopy, thick cable-like flexible edge. The Cable Cast On sets your first row and it contains your very first knitted row.

WHEN: Recommended for items where the first row needs to be firm and it will be in prominent view as in the cast on for hats.

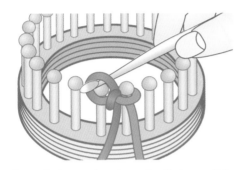

1

Make a slip knot; place it on the first peg. Take the working yarn to the outside of the loom. Using a crochet hook, insert the tip through the slip knot on starting peg, hooking the working yarn and forming a loop. Place the loop made on the adjacent peg to the left.

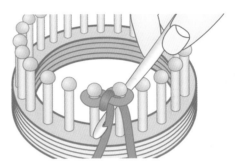

2

With the crochet hook go below the traveling yarn (between the first peg and second peg wrapped), hook the working yarn and pull towards the inside of the loom and towards the third peg. Place the loop from the hook on the next adjacent empty peg (peg 3) and repeat this all around the loom.

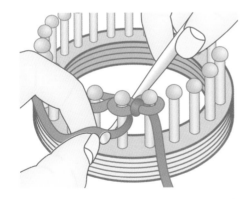

3

When you reach the last peg, place that last loop formed on the first peg. Note how the front of each peg has two loops, while the inside only shows one. E-wrap the first peg with the working yarn. Knit over the two lowest strands off the peg, leaving only one loop on the peg.

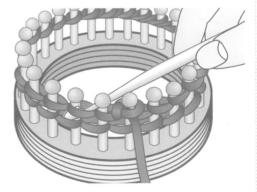

4

Knit over the bottommost loop on all the remaining pegs on the loom. The loom is now ready to be worked in the desired pattern stitch.

More Cast Ons cont.

Chain Cast on

It provides a neat, flexible, non-loopy, crochet-like edge. It is similar to the cable cast on, except for its flexibility. WHEN: It is a good overall cast on.

It is also used when an item calls for cast on stitches at the beginning or end of the next row on flat panels.

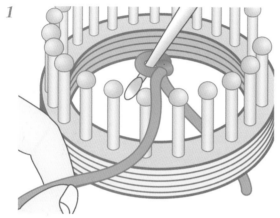

1

Form a slip knot with your yarn. Insert crochet hook through slip knot with the hook towards the center of the knitting loom and the working yarn on the outside of the loom.

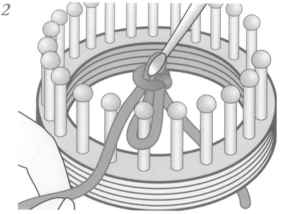

2

Place hook between first two pegs. Hook the working yarn and pull the working yarn through the slip knot that is on the crochet hook (thus, wrapping the post of the peg).

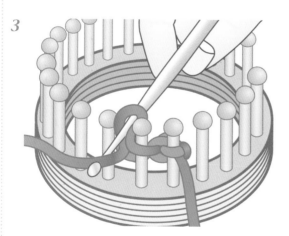

3

With crochet hook towards the inside of the loom, move up between the next set of pegs (between the second and third peg) and repeat step 2, continuing all around the loom.

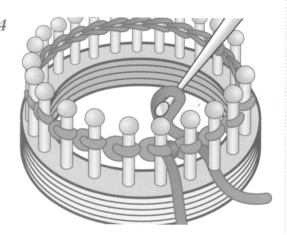

4

When you reach the last peg, take the loop on the hook and place it on the first peg. Knitting loom is ready to be knitted on.

Knit and Purl

The two basic stitches are the knit, or plain, and purl stitches. With these two techniques under your belt you will be able to create numerous stitch pattern for your loom knits.

Knit Stitch (k st)

The knit stitch is the cornerstone of any loom-knitted item. Known also as the flat or plain stitch, the knit stitch resembles the knit stitch created on knitting needles. It looks like a small V.

Preparation: Knitting loom must have at least one stitch on each peg (cast-on row).

1

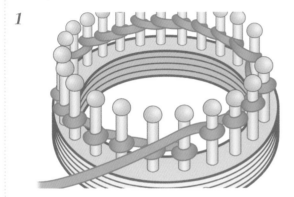

Lay the working yarn in front and above the stitch on the peg.

2

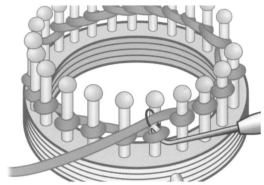

Insert the knitting tool through the stitch on the peg from bottom up. You are going to hook the working yarn where indicated by the red ring.

3

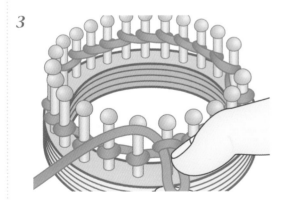

Hook the working yarn with knitting tool, making a loop. Grab the loop with your fingers.

4

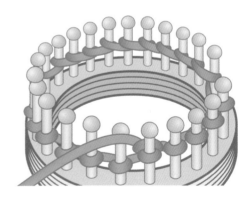

Take the original loop off the peg and replace with the new. Gently tighten the working yarn. Repeat steps 1–4 to complete a knit row.

Knit and Purl cont.

Purl Stitch (p st)

The purl stitch is the reverse of a knit stitch and shows as a small horizontal bump on the front.

In preparation the knitting loom must have at least one stitch on each peg (a cast-on row).

1

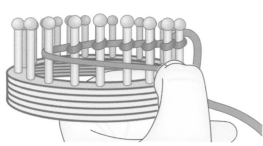

Lay the working yarn in front of and below the stitch on the peg.

2

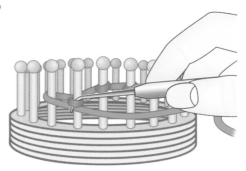

Insert the knitting tool from top to bottom through the stitch on the peg and scoop up the working yarn with the knitting tool.

3

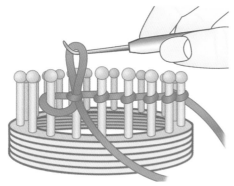

Pull the working yarn through the stitch on the peg to form a loop. Hold the new loop with your fingers.

4

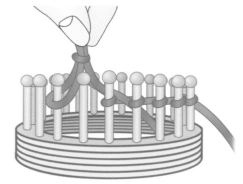

Take the old loop off the peg and place the new loop on the peg. Tug gently on the working yarn to tighten the stitch.
Repeat 1–4 to complete a purl row.

Knit and Purl Combinations

Below you will find a small selection of basic knit and purl combinations. The patterns are written for flat panel and circular knitting, as well as in chart form.

Stockinette Stitch (St st)
Multiple of 1 stitch

The stockinette stitch pattern provides a flat fabric with a smooth right side and a bumpy wrong side.

When knitting in stockinette stitch your knitting will curl at the edges. It is the nature of the stitch to curl. To prevent curling, knit a ribbed or garter stitch edging.

How to: Knit every row/round				
4	K	K	K	K
	K	K	K	K	3
2	K	K	K	K
	K	K	K	K	1

Reverse Stockinette (rev St st)
Multiple of 1 stitch

The reverse stockinette stitch provides a textured fabric with a bumpy right side and a smooth wrong side.

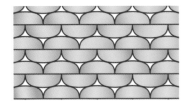

Circular and Flat Knitting:
St st: Knit every round/row
Rev St st: Purl every round/row.

4	P	P	P	P
	P	P	P	P	3
2	P	P	P	P
	P	P	P	P	1

Garter Stitch (g st)
Multiple of 1 stitch

The Garter Stitch produces a reversible fabric—both sides of the knitted item will look the same. The two rows together will show on your knitted item as 1 row of horizontal bumps. Count each row of horizontal bumps as 2 knitted rows but 1 row of garter stitch.

4	P	P	P	P
	K	K	K	K	3
2	P	P	P	P
	K	K	K	K	1

Circular knitting:
Round 1: Purl the entire round.
Round 2: Knit the entire round.
Repeat rounds 1–2.

Flat Knitting:
Row 1: Knit to end.
Row 2: Purl to end.
Repeat Rows 1–2.

Knit and Purl Combinations cont.

Rib Stitch (rib)

The rib stitch produces a reversible fabric with vertical columns of stitches. It is a stretchable stitch, recommended for use whenever a snug fit is required, as in cuffs, sweater hems, necklines.

There are many variations of the rib stitch; presented below are some of the most commonly used.

1 x 1 rib stitch. Multiple of 2 stitches. Knitting Loom must have an even number of pegs.
Circular Knitting:
Row/Rnd 1: *K1, p1. Repeat from * to end of row/rnd. **Consequent rows:** Repeat row 1. (knit the knits, purl the purls)

Flat Panel Knitting:
Row 1: *K1, p1; repeat from * to end.
Row 2: *P1, k1; repeat from * to end.

4	P	K	P	K	
	P	K	P	K	3
2	P	K	P	K	
	P	K	P	K	1

2 x 2 rib stitch. Multiple of 4 stitches + 2

4	P	P	K	K	
	P	P	K	K	3
2	P	P	K	K	
	P	P	K	K	1

Moss Stitch

Multiple of 2: Worked over 2 rows.
Also known as seed stitch, moss stitch provides you with a textured, reversible fabric.

HOW TO:
Flat Knitting:
Row 1–2: *K1, p1, rep from * to the end.

Repeat these 2 rows.
Circular Knitting:
Round 1: *K1, p1, rep from * to the end.
Round 2: *P1, k1, rep from * to the end.

2	K	P	K	P	
	P	K	P	K	1

Double Moss Stitch

Multiple of 2: Worked over 4 rows.
Double Moss stitch is a richly textured stitch, often seen on baby blankets or in combination with cables. It produces a reversible fabric.

HOW TO:
Flat Knitting:
Row 1 and 4: *K1, p1, repeat from * to the end.
Row 2 and 3: *P1, k1, repeat from * to the end.

Circular Knitting:
Round 1 and 2: *K1, p1, repeat from * to the end of the round. **Round 3 and 4:** *P1, k1, repeat from * to the end of the round.
Repeat these 4 rows.

4	K	P	K	P	
	K	P	K	P	3
2	P	K	P	K	
	P	K	P	K	1

Garter Stitch Hat

Put the new stitches you have learnt into practice with this easy to make hat. A little different from the previous project, and later on you can make the scarf to match.

You will need

Knitting Loom

Adult large gauge knitting loom [Round Green Knifty Knitter was used in sample]

Yarn

70 yds (64 m) of super bulky weight yarn [Rowan Big Wool, 100% wool, 87 yds. (79 m) per 100 g, Bohemian used in sample]

Tools

Knitting tool
Tapestry needle
Stitch holder

Size

Fits up to a 20 ins. (51 cm) head

Gauge

8 sts and 12 rows to 4 ins. (10 cm)

Pattern notes

Knitted in the round
Knit refers to the Knit Stitch/Flat Stitch

Note: If you would like to knit this hat and have a looser fit, knit the Single Stitch instead of the Knit Stitch.

Hat Body:

Cast on using the chain method.

Round 1: Knit.
Round 2: Purl.
Repeat rows 1–2 until hat measures 8 ins. (20 cm) from cast-on edge.

Crown Decreases

Divide the stitches on the loom into 4 groups of 9 stitches. Each group will be worked separately.

Row 1: Move the first stitch at each end of this wedge over to the 2nd peg. Knit All the stitches. Knit 2 over 1 on the end pegs.
Row 2: Purl.
Repeat rows 1–2 until you have only 1 stitch left on the wedge. Break yarn leaving a 14 ins. (36 cm)

tail. Place the last stitch remaining from the wedge on a stitch holder.

Attach yarn at the first peg of the next wedge to be worked and repeat wedge instructions.

Closing the Crown

Seam the sides using the yarn tail end from each of the wedges using mattress stitch.

Bind Off

Once all the sides have been seamed, thread the tapestry needle with yarn and pass it through the four stitches on the stitch holder, cinch it closed with the Gathering Removal Method. Pass the needle to the reverse side of the hat and weave in yarn ends.

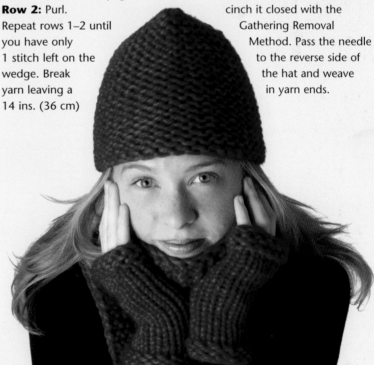

Binding off

Although it is the last step in creating the garment, binding off holds as much importance as any other part of the knitted item and has impact on how the final item will look.

Single Crochet Bind Off

The single crochet bind-off gathers the stitches together for a tapered edge. Recommended on sleeves that require a firm edge.

1

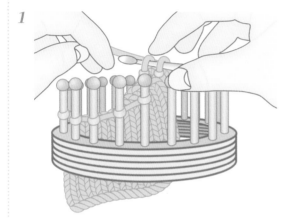

Use a crochet hook, the size recommended for your yarn. Start at the side where the working yarn is located. With the working yarn on the left, and crochet hook on the right, remove the stitch from the peg with the crochet hook.

2

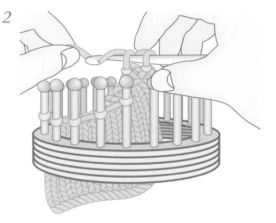

Hook the working yarn with the crochet hook; pull the yarn through the stitch to make a loop.

3

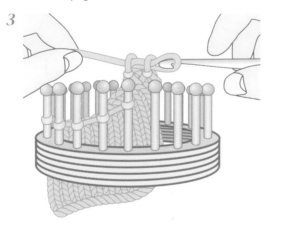

Repeat 1–2 into the next stitches, making sure to pass the new loop formed through both the stitch being bound off and the stitch on the hook.

4

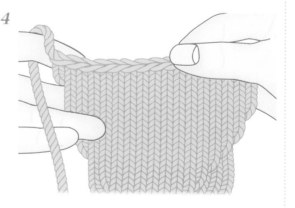

When you reach the last stitch, cut the working yarn leaving a 5-inch (12.5 cm) tail, hook the tail and pass it through the last stitch to lock it in place.

Double Crochet Bind Off

Here you crochet one chain between each loop removed from the knitting loom. It provides a firm, non-tapered edge, recommended for items that require a flexible finish. Using the hook size recommended for your yarn, start at the side where the working yarn is located.

1

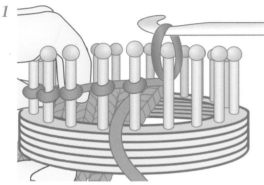

With working yarn in your left hand, and crochet hook in your right, remove the stitch off the peg with the crochet hook.

2

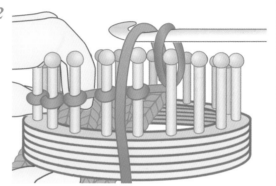

Hook the working yarn with the crochet hook; pull the yarn through the stitch on the hook to make a loop

3

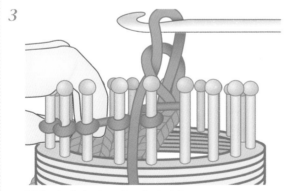

Make 1 chain (crochet 1 chain).

4

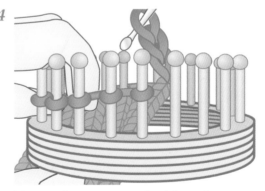

Move to the next peg to the right and repeat steps 1–3. When you reach the last stitch, cut the working yarn leaving a 5-inch (12.5 cm) tail, hook the tail and pass it through the last stitch to lock it in place.

Binding off cont.

Sewn Bind Off

This is a good overall bind off method to know. The edging will match most cast-on edges. In preparation, cut the working yarn leaving a tail length of yarn about three times the width of the knitted item. Thread tapestry needle through the yarn and follow the steps below.

1

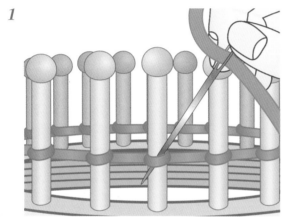

Pass the needle through the first stitch by inserting the needle from top to bottom

2

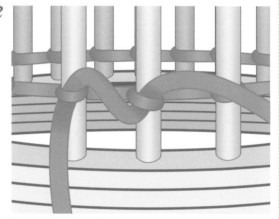

Pass the needle through the second stitch by inserting the needle from top to bottom.

3

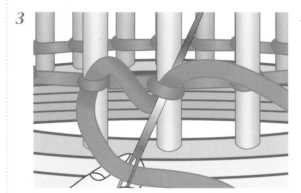

Insert the needle through the first stitch by inserting the needle from bottom to top.

4

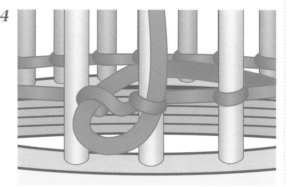

Take the stitch off the peg.
Repeat 1–4 until there is only one stitch on the loom. Pass the needle through the stitch from bottom to top. Take stitch off the peg.

Linking Bind Offs

Sometimes you will need to join two panels together while binding off. Below are two methods, one involves using knitting needles and the other is done on a knitting loom.

Three-needle Bind Off

Preparation: Obtain 3 knitting needles or 2 knitting needles and 1 crochet hook. Transfer the stitches from the knitting loom onto one of the knitting needles. Transfer the stitches from the other panel to the second knitting needle. Hold the two needles together, right sides together. The two knitting needles should be held in one hand together, both pointing in the same direction.

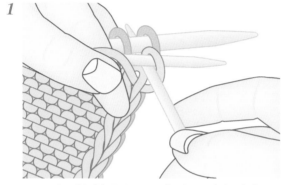

1

Insert the third knitting needle through both first stitches and knit them together.

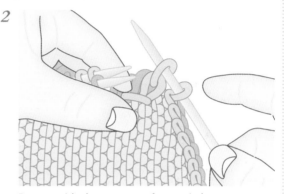

2

Repeat with the next set of two stitches.

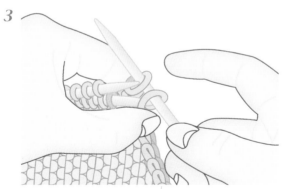

3

Pass the first stitch on the right knitting needle over the second stitch—1 stitch bound off.

With Crochet Hook

1 Insert the crochet hook through both first stitches (front needle and back needle), hook the working yarn and pull through the two stitches.
2 Repeat with the next set of two stitches.
3 Pass the front stitch through the back stitch— 1 stitch bound off.

Repeat 1–3 until all stitches have been bound off. Cut working yarn and pull through the last stitch.

Grafting

Another useful linking method known as Kitchener stitch, or grafting, is often used on the toe of socks as it doesn't create an uncomfortable ridge.
You will need two knitting needles, set up as step 1 above. Cut the working yarn keeping a long tail, and thread the end through a tapestry needle.

1 Take the yarn through the first stitch on the needle closest to you as if to purl, then through the first stitch on the second needle, as if you were going to knit it.
2 Slip these two stitches off their needles, and repeat step 1 until you reach the end of the rows.
3 Gently pull the yarn to tighten the stitch, but don't pull too much.
4 Weave in the ends to the wrong side.

Linking Bind-offs cont.

Joining Two Panels on a Knitting Loom

1

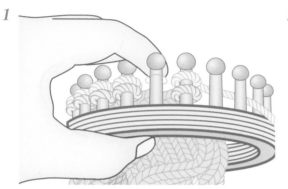

Remove panels from knitting loom and place the stitches on a stitch holder. Place one of the panels back on the knitting loom with the right side facing the inside of the knitting loom; the wrong side will be facing you. Pay close attention to putting the stitches back on the knitting loom correctly.

3

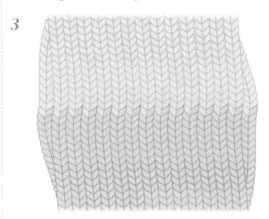

Follow the Basic Bind Off method and bind off the stitches—knit through both stitches on the pegs (lay working yarn above the two stitches on the peg, insert knitting tool through the two stitches, catch the working yarn and pull through the two stitches, hold the loop formed by the working yarn, take the two stitches off the peg and place the newly formed loop on the peg).

2

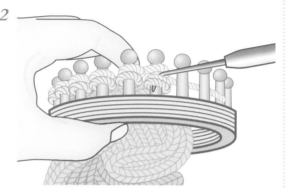

Place the second panel on the knitting loom by placing the stitches on the same pegs that the first panel is occupying, right sides of the panels together.

Mattress Stitch

Once you are loom knitting flat panels you will need to join your seams. Mattress stitch is a neat stitch, which can hardly be seen from the right side. It is advisable to use the same yarn that you knitted with, unless you want the stitches to be a feature of your work.

1 Lay the pieces to be joined, right side up and side-by-side. Thread a tapestry needle with the tail end. Bring the yarn through to the front, in the middle of the first stitch on the first row of the seam. Take the needle through to the same position on the other piece, and bring it out in the middle of the edge stitch one row up.

2 Insert the needle back into the first piece of fabric, in the same place that the yarn last came out. Then bring the needle out in the middle of the stitch above. Repeat this making a zig-zag seam from edge to edge for a few more rows. You can pull the thread firmly, and the stitches almost disappear. When the seam is finished, weave in the ends.

Making I-Cords on a Loom

Cords can be made on spools, or any circular knitting loom that is small enough to be worked like a small spool knitter, or you can create I-cords by using a round loom as a rake.

3-Stitch I-cord

Notes:
- I-cord is knitted with the Knit Stitch.
- Work the loom in a clockwise direction (right to left).

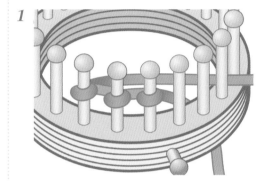

1. Cast on 3 pegs. With working yarn coming from the third peg run the yarn behind the pegs to the first peg.

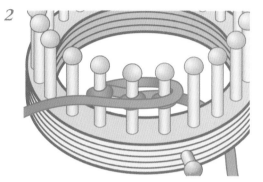

2. Bring yarn to the front of the loom and knit the 3 pegs.

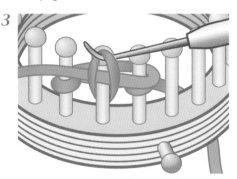

3. Knit the second peg, then the first, and the third last. Repeat until the cord measures the desired length.

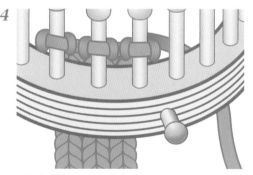

4. Bind off by cutting the yarn leaving a 4-inch (10 cm) tail. Move the loop from second to first peg. Knit over. Move the loop on peg 1 to peg 2. Move the loop on peg 3 to peg 2. Knit over. With working yarn, e-wrap peg 2. Knit over. Pull the last loop off the peg and pull on the yarn tail end.

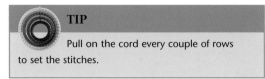

TIP
Pull on the cord every couple of rows to set the stitches.

I-Cord Hot Pad

Making I-cords is seriously addictive. Once you have got the bug, you will have to find something to do with all those cords! Here's one idea; you are sure to have more.

You will need

Knitting Loom

Large gauge knitting loom with at least 3 pegs

Yarn

40 yards of bulky weight yarn
[Manos Del Uruguay, hand-spun 100% wool, 137 yds. (125 m) per 100g skein was used in sample]

Tools

Knitting Tool
Tapestry needle

Instructions

Make a 3 foot (92 cm) long I-cord and fasten off.

Place it on a flat surface and coil it around in a circle. Sew the I-cord sides together with the same yarn and a tapestry needle. Start at the center on the back and work to the end, weaving in any yarn ends, to make a woolly mat. Wool is naturally heat-resistant and washable and so is hygenic for use in the kitchen.

TIP

This project uses the 3-stitch I-cord. To make a thicker, or thinner I-cord, simply cast on additional or fewer stitches and follow the instructions on the previous page.

Dropped it... Fixing Mistakes

So you have been happily knitting, then you look down and horror, you see a stitch dangling all by itself. What do you do? If it is one or two stitches, we can save the day.

Picking up a Dropped Stitch

As soon as you spot the dropped stitch, hold it in place with a safety pin or stitch holder; failure to do so will cause the stitch to drop further down the column. Knit to the peg next to the dropped stitch. Now the scary part: unravel the stitch on the same column where the dropped stitch is located; it will stop unraveling when you reach the dropped stitch. Then get a crochet hook...

On Stockinette side fabric

1

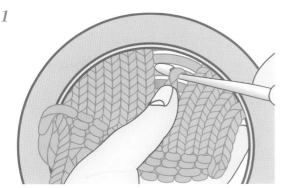

Insert the crochet hook from front to back through the stitch dropped.

2

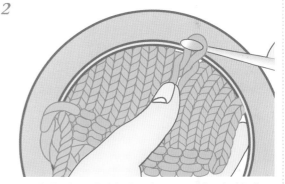

Hook the first "ladder" or horizontal bar behind the stitch and pull it through the stitch to the front of the work.

3

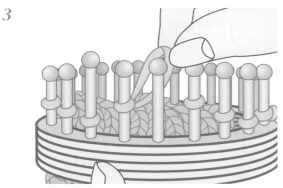

Continue picking up the unraveled stitches by following Step 2. When all stitches have been picked up, place the last stitch back on the peg.

On Purl side fabric

1 Insert crochet hook through the back side of the fabric (inside the circle of the loom, or the wrong side of the fabric). Hook the dropped stitch.
2 Hook the unraveled strand behind the stitch and pull it through the stitch to the back of the fabric.
3 Continue picking up the unraveled stitches by following Step 2. When all stitches have been picked up, place the last stitch back on the peg.

Fixing Mistakes cont.

Fixing Stitches

If you accidentally knitted the wrong stitch on the row below, you have two options:

Option 1: Tink back the row, one stitch at a time, until you reach the stitch where the mistake is located. Fix the stitch and continue knitting.

Option 2: Drop the stitch on that column of stitches and fix the mistake.

> **GLOSSARY**
>
> **Tink** is the process of undoing a row by undoing a stitch at a time—it is the word knit spelled backwards.

If the problem is located a few rows back, it is best to unravel the knitting and undo the entire row with the mistake.

1 Use a piece of waste yarn or a circular needle to hold your stitches to act as a lifeline one row below the problem row.

2 Take the stitches off the pegs and unravel all the stitches until you reach the row with the lifeline that is your stitch holder.

3 Place the stitches back on the pegs. Make sure to position the stitches on the loom the correct way. Twist them if you were knitting the Twisted Knit Stitch. Don't twist them if you were knitting the Knit Stitch.

Joining Yarns

When you least expect it, it happens—the yarn suddenly comes to an end, or worse, breaks. It is time to attach a new yarn to the project.

At the Edge: Join the new yarn at the beginning of a row. If possible join the yarn on an edge that will be within a seam.

Method 1: Leave at tail of about 5–6 inches (12–15 cm) in length on the old skein and another tail the same length on the new skein. Hold the two yarns together and knit the first three stitches. Drop the old skein and continue knitting with the newly joined yarn.

Method 2: Leave a tail of about 5–6 inches (12–15 cm) in length on the old skein and another tail the same length on the new skein. Tie a temporary knot with the two ends as close to the project as possible. Pick up the newly

joined yarn and continue knitting. When project is complete, go back and undo the knot, weave in the ends in the opposite direction to close the gap formed by the change of yarns.

Stuck in the Middle: Occasionally you will need to join yarn in the middle of a row. In this case, you can use Option 2 above. Tie a temporary knot close to the garment; make sure to leave a 5–6 inch (12–15 cm) tail on both ends. Continue knitting from the new yarn. Make sure to undo the knot before weaving in the ends.

> **TIP**
>
> If you encounter a knot in your yarn, do not knit with it. Cut it and join the yarn using one of the methods above.

Creating Flat Panels

Don't feel intimidated by the idea of creating a flat panel on a circular loom. It is a simple process that involves knitting on the knitting loom in a "C" figure.

From A to B and back again...

Knitting a flat panel on the knitting loom is not much different from knitting circularly on the knitting loom. You can do the same cast on methods, knit the same stitches, and use the same bind off methods.

However, there are a few things that differ. Since you are not knitting circularly around the knitting loom, you will have a starting point and an ending point. At both ends you will have a turning peg/stitch marking the beginning of a new row or the end of the last one.

When starting at point A, the peg at point A is your beginning peg. The peg at point B becomes your last peg, and will also be your turning peg. When you finish a row, by knitting the peg at point B, you turn and knit back to point A. Thus the pegs and Point A and B alternate as turning pegs and beginning and ending pegs for the rows.

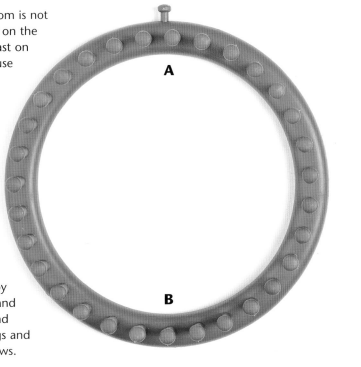

Beware of the Selvedge

Now you are no longer going round in circles, you will have edges to deal with. The edge stitches of a knitted panel are called edge or selvedge stitches.

When knitting from a pattern, look for instructions on how to treat the selvedge stitches. One way is to wrap the turning pegs and knit them, as above. Alternatively you can slip stitch the first stitch on each row.

A slip stitch (sl st) is simply a stitch that is not knitted. You skip the peg and simply take the yarn to the next peg and knit it. Using a slip stitch at the beginning of each row creates a chain-like edge at both sides of the knitted item.

How to decide which turning option to use? If you are going to be seaming two pieces together or adding a border, it is best to knit the edge stitches (always knit the first and last stitches). If you are looking for a more decorative edging, slip the first stitch of every row. However, slipping the stitch on each row will deduct the width of your knitted item by two stitches. If the pattern doesn't allow for this, you will have to add one stitch to either side of the pattern as you go along.

GLOSSARY

Selvedge As its name suggests, this is the self-made edge of the fabric you are creating, sometimes disappearing in a seam, but sometimes a more visible finished edge.

Turning stitch options

You can knit the first peg, or slip it. Knitting the Knit Stitch or the Twisted Knit stitch at the beginning and end of each row provides a nice even edge.

To begin, cast on your knitting loom in a clockwise direction. The practice project uses the slip method at the selvedge. You will see the difference.

Using the Twisted Knit Stitch

1

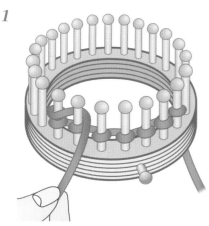

E-wrap the last peg in a counter clockwise direction, run the working yarn behind to the next peg and wrap around it in a clockwise direction. Knit over this stitch, then go back and knit over on the first peg. Tug on the yarn gently to tighten the first stitch.

2

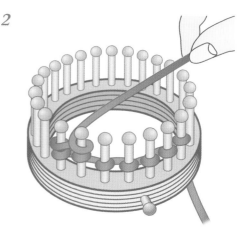

Continue knitting back to the next pegs in a clockwise direction. When you reach the last peg on the right, knit it, then bring working yarn to the front of the peg. Wrap around it in a clockwise direction. Bring working yarn behind the pegs.

3

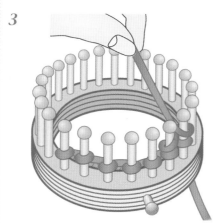

E-wrap the next peg in a counterclockwise direction. Knit over. Go back to the first peg and knit the stitch. Tug gently on the working yarn to tighten the first stitch.

4

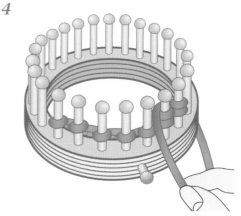

Continue knitting down the loom, e-wrapping the pegs in a counterclockwise direction.

Purple Trendy Scarf

Grab a ball of some funky, novelty yarn and knit an extraordinary flat panel scarf. The Purple Trendy Scarf knits up quickly on a large gauge knitting loom.

You will need

Knitting Loom

Large gauge knitting loom with at least 12 pegs
[Red Knifty Knitter used in sample]

Yarn

90 yards (82 m) bulky weight novelty yarn
[Jo-Ann Sensations Halo, 100% nylon, 49.21 yds. (45 m) per 1.75 ozs (50 g) ball used in sample]

Tools

Tapestry needle
Knitting tool

Size

4 x 44 ins. (10 x 112 cm)

Pattern notes

Knitted completely as a flat panel
Selvedge stitches slipped thru'out
k=knit stitch/flat stitch

Instructions

Cast on 12 stitches.
Row 1: Sl1, k11.
Row 2: Sl1, p11.
Repeat Rows 1–2 until item measures 30 ins. (76 cm).

Divide scarf for keyhole opening:
Attach a second ball of yarn

to the seventh peg.
Next row: Sl1, k5.
Pick up the new yarn attached to peg 7 and knit to peg 12.
Next row: Sl1, p5. Drop yarn and pick up the other skein of yarn and purl to peg 12.
Repeat above 2 rows 3 times.
Rejoin the two sides. Remove one of the balls and work entire row with one strand.

Next row: Sl1, k11.
Next row: Sl1, p11.
Repeat Rows 1–2 until item measures 44 ins. (112 cm) from cast on edge.
Bind off with basic removal method.

To wear, pass one of the sides through the opening or wrap anyhow the mood takes you.

Shaping

When making most things shaping will be necessary and is achieved by creating increases and decreases in the number of stitches in your knitted items.

Increases (inc)

Adding extra stitches to the panel makes it wider. When increases happen within rows, it is recommended to only increase 2 stitches on a given row. Increases are used to shape items such as sweater sleeves, skirts, and items that fan out. There are various ways to increase stitches on the loom, and all of them require you to move the stitches outwards to the empty pegs to allow room, or an empty peg, for the new stitch. Below, you will find three methods. Familiarize yourself with all three.

Make 1 (M1)

1

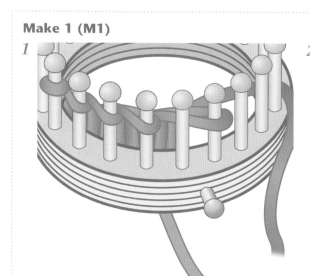

2

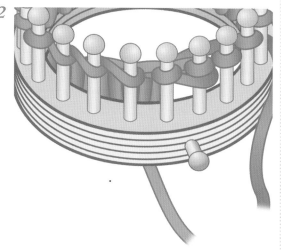

Move the last stitch to the next empty peg outwards, leaving an empty peg between the last peg and the peg before last.

Make 1 (M1). Knit the stitches on the knitting loom, when you reach the empty peg, e-wrap it and continue knitting to the end of the row. Increasing in this manner, will leave a small hole where the increase was created.

> **TIP**
>
> When creating a piece that will require many increases, make sure to cast on to a loom that is big enough to hold all the stitches you'll need.

Smart shaping

As a new loom knitter, the tendency will be to simply cast on the desired number of additional stitches at the end of the row rather than increase within the row. By increasing within the row, the knitted item maintains its edge shaping.

The increasing techniques here are recommended whenever you need to increase one or two stitches within a row. Casting on is recommended when increasing more than two stitches on the edge of the row. You couldn't make a shape like this fish without increasing and decreasing.

Lifted Increase Make 1

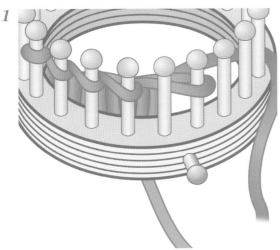

Move the last stitch outwards to the next empty peg, leaving an empty peg between the last peg and the peg before last.

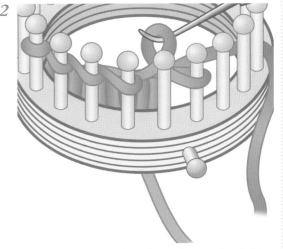

With the knitting tool reach for the running-ladder coming from the two stitches on either side below the empty peg. Twist the strand and place it on the empty peg (if you don't twist it, you will create a small hole). Knit your row as usual.

Row Below

This is another way of increasing using a crochet hook.

1 Move the last stitch to the next empty peg outwards, leaving an empty peg between the last peg and the peg before last. Get a crochet hook.

2 Knit to the empty peg, and with the crochet hook reach one stitch below (on the wrong side), pass the hook through one of the "legs" of the stitch and hook the working yarn making a loop. Place the loop on the empty peg. Make sure to not pull on the stitch below too much as this may cause the stitch to pull together.

Decreases (dec)

Removing stitches from your panel will make the panel narrower. When decreases happen within rows it is recommended to decrease 1 or 2 stitches in from either edge to keep the selvedge neat. There are various ways to decrease on the knitting loom; all of them require you to move the stitches inwards. Familiarize yourself with the methods below.

Knit 2 Together

Knitting 2 together (k2tog) creates a right slanting decrease, and is best created at the beginning of a knit row.

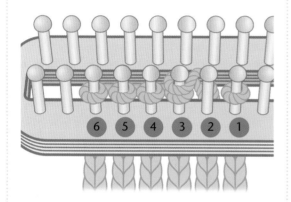

Move the stitch from peg 2 to peg 3 (the peg to its left). Peg 3 now has two stitches and peg 2 is empty.
Note: the stitch from peg 3 will be on the bottom and the stitch from peg 2 is on top. When knitting over, the stitch that was on peg 2 will disappear behind the stitch from peg 3.
Move stitches inwards so there are no empty pegs. Knit the row as usual, making sure to knit 2 over 1 on the peg with the extra stitch.

Slip, Slip Knit

The left slanting decrease is the mirror image of a k2tog and is achieved by a Slip, Slip Knit (ssk) at the end of a row.

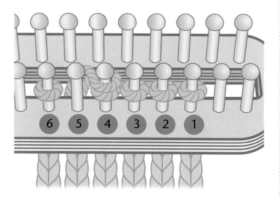

Move the stitch from peg 5 over to peg 4 (or the peg to its right).
Note: The stitch from the right peg (peg 4) is on the bottom, the stitch from the left peg (peg 5) is on top—do not change the order of the loops— keep the bottom loop on the bottom and the top on the top. Move stitches inwards so there are no empty pegs. Continue knitting as usual down the row.

Purl 2 together

Also known as p2tog, this too creates a right slanting decrease, best created at the beginning of a purl side row. It is made just like the k2tog above, except in a purl row.
Purl the row as usual. When you reach the peg with the extra stitch, lay the yarn below the two loops, and purl them, making sure to remove the two loops off the peg and leaving the newly formed loop.

TIP

It is best to do all increases/decreases at least one or two stitches away from the edge. Creating the increases/decreases right on the edge can cause sloppy edges and it makes picking up stitches very difficult.

Increasing two stitches or more

In certain cases, a pattern will call for increasing more than two stitches at any given row. In this case, it is best to cast on the stitches using a method like the Chain Cast on Method (see page 40).

Increasing more than two stitches at the beginning of the row:

1 Knit the entire row as called for in the pattern. With the working yarn coming from the last stitch, cast on to the empty pegs using the chain cast on method. When you reach the desired peg number, stop.

2 The loom is threaded with the extra stitches and is now ready. Turn back and knit or purl these stitches as directed by the pattern.

Decreasing two stitches or more

A pattern sometimes will ask you to bind off stitches at a certain point within the pattern.

Knit to the stitch where the binding off is supposed to begin. Start bind off using the Basic Bind Off Method (see page 33), stop when you have bound off the number of stitches called for in pattern.

Most patterns will let you know which increase or decrease method you should use. If there is no information about which method to use, knit a small swatch and experiment with the different methods above and see which one looks best. The increases on a sleeve, for example, usually come in pairs—k2tog at the beginning of the row and ssk at the end—look for these mirror images whenever you are knitting something that has increases or decreases at each end.

Short Row Shaping

This allows shaping a knitted panel without the decreasing stitches. It creates soft curves by knitting a row to a certain stitch in the row, then turning back and knitting in the other direction. It is a method commonly used in heels, blouse darts for the stomach or bust area, and in any other item where you want seamless curves. Shaping with short rows has one pitfall that you must be aware of. It is necessary to wrap the stitch after the turning point to avoid a hole between the turning stitch and the next stitch. The "wrap" eliminates this almost completely.

How to Wrap and Turn (W&T)

When knitting each wrapped peg, lift both the wrap and the stitch together, 2 over 1, as this will eliminate the wrap and fill the hole made with the short rows.

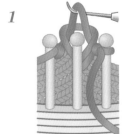

1

Knit or purl to the desired turning stitch. Take the stitch off the next peg and hold it with your knitting tool.

2

Wrap the peg by taking the yarn towards the inside of the loom and wrapping around the peg. The working yarn will end up to the front of the knitting loom.

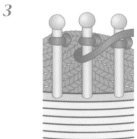

3

Place the stitch back on the peg. Take the working yarn and knit or purl back across the row.

Rainbow Fish Pillow

Learn the basics of increasing and decreasing on a flat panel by creating a cute bedroom pillow for a child.

You will need

Knitting Loom

Regular gauge knitting loom with at least 20 pegs

Yarn

100 yds. (91.5 m) of bulky weight yarn [1 ball Berroco Air, 78% Wool, 22% Nylon, 115 yds (106 m) to 1.75 oz (50 g) was used in sample]

Other

Button for eye
Polyester batting for stuffing

Tools

Knitting Tool
Tapestry needle

Pattern notes

Item is knit as a flat panel
K=Knit=Knit Stitch/Flat Stitch
P=Purl
Inc 1= increase 1 stitch with the lifted increase method
SSK= slip, slip, knit = left slanting decrease
k2tog = knit 2 together = right slanting decrease

Stitch Pattern—Garter Stitch (gs):
Row 1: Knit.
Row 2: Purl.

Instructions

Make 2
Cast on 20 stitches with cable cast on method.
Row 1: P.
Row 2: K2, k2tog, k to last 4 sts, ssk, k2.
Row 3: P.
Row 4: K.
Rep Rows 1–4 until you have 6 stitches remaining.
Knit 2 rows of garter stitch.

Row 1: P.
Row 2: K2, inc 1, k to last 2 sts, inc 1, k2.
Row 3: P.
Row 4: K.
Rep Rows 1–4 until 20 stitches are on the loom.
Knit 8 rows of garter stitch. You should have 16 rows in total.

Row 1: P.
Row 2: K2, k2tog, k to last 4 sts, ssk, k2.
Row 3: P.
Row 4: K.
Rep Rows 1–4 until you have 6 sts remaining.
Knit 1 row of garter stitch.
Bind off.

Assembly

Fix a button to represent the eye using tapestry needle and matching yarn. Sew and stuff the body of the fish.

Caution: If knitting this item for a baby—embroider an eye instead of attaching the button.

Working with Color

It is easy to jazz up a simple pattern by doing color changes along the way. Take a chance and create a wild project with some odd skeins left from other projects.

Stripes

Creating stripes is the easiest method to spice up a project. Knitting with stripes allows you to use as many colors as you wish without having to carry more than one color at a time within the row.

Designing with stripes is easy—gather all your odd skeins and sit down and loom knit a one-of-a-kind item.

Keep the following in suggestions in mind when creating your stripes:
• Wide stripes
• Narrow stripes
• Alternate between narrow and wide stripes
• Spice it up: mix wild colors and textured yarns

Stripy Goodness

Now that you have gathered all your odd skeins, it is time to sit down and knit your original item. Your one-of-a-kind creation will have one main color (MC) with one (or more) contrasting colors (CC). When more than one contrasting color is used, the colors are designated letters, such as A, B, C, D, and so on.

Knit a few rows with your main color. When it's time to change to a new color, join the new yarn at the beginning of a row (See Joining Yarn on page 54).

After you have your desired colors set up, you can carry the color along the edge of the item if knitting thin stripes. If you are knitting wider stripes, cut the yarn at the end of a row, and join yarns at the beginning of a row.

When Flat Panel knitting, try to work the stripes in sets of two rows, then the yarn ends on the same side. If you work an uneven number of rows, you will find your yarn on the opposite side of your knitting and you will have to cut the yarn and join the yarn to the opposite edge.

Weaving the Ends

Weave in the ends vertically along the edge of the item—through the same color stripe as the yarn being woven. You can also weave in the ends to the wrong side of the item.

Going Up

Creating thin vertical stripes is simple, and weaving of yarns at the back of the work is not required. The unused yarn can be carried behind the work. To create thin vertical stripes, you will need yarn in two colors: a main color (MC) and a contrasting color (CC).

1 Pick up the main color and knit the stitches you desire in the main color, skip the ones you desire in contrasting color.

2 Go back to the beginning of the row, pick up the contrasting color and knit all the pegs skipped in Step 1.

Repeat steps 1–2 throughout.

Weaving the Ends

Weave in the ends vertically along the edge of the item—through the same color stripe as the yarn being woven.

Painting with yarn

The art of Fair Isle loom knitting is a technique of multicolored knitting, where a row is worked with only two colors in small repeating sections of color patterns.

Traditional Fair Isle knitting is done completely in stockinette stitch (knit every row in the round), two different colors per row, and the items are usually circular. The circular nature of the item helps to hide the floats created by the color changes within the row. When carrying the unused color, it is recommended to not carry it over more than 5–7 sts, or 1–1.5 inches (2.5–4 cm).

Fair Isle patterns are usually depicted in chart form and share some characteristics with regular knitting charts. Each square represents a stitch. The squares will either be colored in or will have a color symbol and key.

For Flat Panel knitting: Read the chart starting at the bottom, right side. Then move up to the second row, and read it from left to right. For circular knitting: Read the chart starting at the bottom, right side. Continue reading the next rounds starting at the right side.

Loom Knitting Fair Isle

Although it may seem complicated, the process of painting with your yarn is quite simple.

There are two methods that you can use: The first method keeps your yarns separated and untangled. You pick up the main color at the beginning of a row, knit the required stitches then drop it at the end of the row. Pick up the contrasting color and knit all the required stitches with that color, then drop it. In the second method, you carry both yarns with you in your dominant hand as you work the stitch pattern. When the pattern calls for the CC, drop the MC color and

24	23	22	21	20	19	18	17	16	15	14	13	12	11	10	9	8	7	6	5	4	3	2	1	
□	□	□	□	□	□	□	□	□	□	□	□	□	□	□	□	□	□	□	□	□	□	□	□	4
□	□	■	■	■	□	□	□	■	■	■	□	□	□	■	■	■	□	□	□	■	■	■	□	3
□	■	■	■	□	■	□	■	■	■	□	■	□	■	■	■	□	■	□	■	■	■	□	■	2
■	■	■	□	□	□	■	■	■	□	□	□	■	■	■	□	□	□	■	■	■	□	□	□	1

Key

□ **knit** MC

■ **color 1** CC

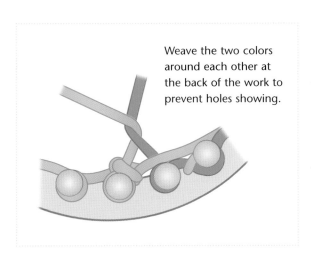

Weave the two colors around each other at the back of the work to prevent holes showing.

bring the CC above the MC working yarn, knit as required. When the pattern calls for the MC, drop the CC, reach below for the MC color. Every time you change yarns, drop the new one above then reach below for the other.

To minimize the length of the floats at the back of the work, it is advisable to weave the yarns around each other when traveling more than three stitches. To weave the yarns around each other: knit a few stitches with the MC color, drop it and pick up the CC, wrap the CC around the MC, drop the CC, pick up the MC and keep on knitting. Take both colors to the back of the work, and twist them together (see diagram above).

Fair Isle allows you to create a wide range of complex color designs. Sit down with some graph paper and different coloring pencils and try different color combinations before trying it on the knitting loom. Have fun painting patterns with your yarn!

Fair Isle Characteristics
- 2 colors per row: main color (MC) and the contrasting color (CC)
- Stockinette stitch
- Wrong side does not show

Practice Project

Winter Hat

The beauty of stranded knitting comes alive with this wintery hat. It depicts a landscape of falling snowflakes. Knitted with a classic, soft merino wool, this hat is sure to keep you warm during the winter months.

You will need

Knitting Loom

Regular gauge round knitting loom with a peg multiple of 12 [Adult regular gauge hat loom by Décor Accents was used in sample]

Yarn

200 yards (183 m) main color 50 yds. (46 m) contrasting color [Patons Classic Merino Wool, 100% Wool, 223 yds. (204 m) per 100 g, was used in sample]

Tools

Knitting tool
Tapestry needle
Five stitch markers
Row counter (optional)

Size

Adult

Gauge

13 sts and 20 rows to 4 ins. (10 cm)

Pattern notes

Use 2 strands of yarn throughout.
MC = Main Color
CC = Contrasting Color
K = knit stitch
P = purl

Snowflake Stitch Pattern:

Multiple of 12

12	11	10	9	8	7	6	5	4	3	2	1	
			■			■				■		9
		■	■		■	■			■		■	8
■	■		■	■	■		■	■			■	7
	■	■		■			■			■		6
	■	■		■			■	■	■		■	5
			■				■		■	■		4
		■					■				■	3
									■	■		2
							■				■	1

Key

☐ **knit** Main Color
■ **color 1** Contrasting Color

Instructions

Place stitch markers 12 spaces apart. Cast on 60 sts in the round with Crochet Chain method and MC.

Rnd 1: *K2, p2; rep from * to the end of round.
Repeat rnd 1 until brim measures 2 ins. from cast on edge.

Knit the 9 rows from chart as follows:

Rnd 1: *K1 with MC, knit 1 with CC, k3 with MC, k1 with CC, k3 with MC, k1 with CC, k2 with MC; rep from * to the end of round.

Rnd 2: *K1 with CC, k1 with MC, k1 with CC, k2 with MC, k2 with CC, k1 with MC, knit 2 with CC, k2 with MC; rep from * to end.

Rnd 3: *K3 with MC, k2 with CC, k1 with MC, k3 with CC, k1 with MC, k2 with CC; rep from * to end.

Rnd 4: *K1 with MC, k1 with CC, k2 with MC, k2 with CC, k1 with MC, k1 with CC, k1 with MC, k2 with CC, k1 with MC; rep from * to end.

Rnd 5: K3 with CC, k2 with MC, k2 with CC, k1 with MC, k2 with CC, k2 with MC.

Rnd 6: *K1 with MC, k1 with CC, k2 with MC, k2 with CC, k1 with MC, k1 with CC, k1 with MC, k2 with CC, k1 with MC; rep from * to the end of round.

Rnd 7: *K3 with MC, k2 with CC, k1 with MC, k3 with CC, k1 with MC, k2 with CC; rep from * to the end of round.

Rnd 8: *K1 with CC, k1 with MC, k1 with CC, k2 with MC, k2 with CC, k1 with MC, k2 with CC, k2 with MC; rep from * to the end of round.

Rnd 9: *K1 with MC, k1 with CC, k3 with MC, k1 with CC, k3 with MC, k1 with CC, k2 with MC; rep from * to the end of round.

Knit in stockinette stitch for 4 ins. (10 cm).

Bind off using the gather removal method.

Sock Loom Knitting

The sock looms are small enough to fit into a small bag and be carried along with you. Once you can knit and purl you can be creating beautiful knitted socks.

Sock Yarn

Yarn comes in different thickness from super chunky down to cobweb lace weight. The knitting loom gauge will determine the thickness of yarn you can use for your socks. There are many yarns that are inexpensive and durable. Visit your local yarn shop and browse through their sock yarn collection to get an idea of the different yarns available.

Did you know that yarn has memory? Items made with yarn that retains memory can return back to their shape after being stretched out. A yarn with good memory, like wool, is great for socks.

Sock Knitting Looms

Virtually any knitting loom that produces the size of tube needed can be used as a sock loom. However, to produce socks that you can wear with everyday shoes, you need a knitting loom with a very small gauge that provides a very tight knit gauge. The socks completed for this book were done on two different gauge looms: the practice project and the Weekend Socks were completed on the Blue Knifty Knitter loom, the Mock Cable Socks were completed on a Décor Accents extra fine gauge sock knitting loom. Whichever knitting loom you choose —enjoy the beauty of handknitting your own socks.

To select the appropriate size knitting loom:

1 Place your foot on a flat surface.

2 Measure around the ball of the foot (the widest part below the toe line).

3 Write down the measurement.

Generally socks are knitted with a negative ease of 10–15%, so try to find a knitting loom that produces a tube 10–15% smaller than the measurement found above.

Cuff

The cuff is the first part of the sock that is knitted. It requires a flexible cast on to allow a comfortable fit—the cable cast on is recommended.

The Anatomy of a Sock

Socks can be knitted either toe up, or top down. All the patterns in this book are for top down socks. The sock is knitted in one single piece; it starts in the round, then it is knitted flat for the heel, then it is knitted in the round again for the foot, and finally the toe is knitted flat, and grafted.

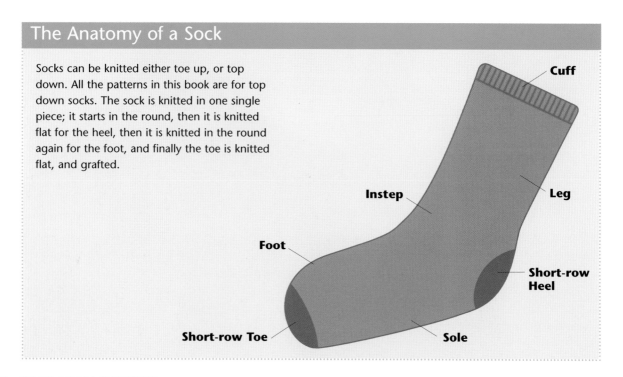

Cuff

Instep

Leg

Foot

Short-row Heel

Short-row Toe

Sole

Memory Yarn

Wool and nylon
Durable and strong with some memory.
Wool
Warm during winter, cool during summer.
Has memory which makes it less likely to stretch out of shape.
Cotton
Cool during the summer. No memory.

Leg
The leg is knitted next and, like the cuff, needs to be flexible, so a combination of ribbing and stockinette stitch is usually used.

Short-row Heel
The heel is where the magic takes place—this small part is where the tube becomes a recognizable sock. The heel is knitted as a flat panel with decreases and increases to form an hourglass shape. The technique of short-row shaping is used to create the decreases.

Foot
Once the heel is completed, the rest is fairly simple. The foot is knitted in the round.

Toe
The toe is another magical part of our sock making technique. In this book's patterns, we will use the same technique and the same numbers used in the heel section to make the toe, what you will have is a little cup that extends from the sole of the sock to the top part of the sock. The one side of the cup will need to be grafted to the top foot part of the sock.

The Short-row Technique
At first, when you begin knitting the heel, it looks like just a small triangle, and then the triangle takes the shape of a small cup. This small magic is what turns a simple tube into a cherished handknit sock.

The heel is created in two parts—a decreasing part and increasing part. The decreasing section requires the knowledge of a technique called wrap and turn (W&T). The increasing section requires the knitter to knit over the wrap and the stitch at the same time.

The term short-row means that a row is not knitted to the end; instead, you will knit to a certain point and stop. Then, you turn back and knit in the other direction. However, if you knit to the designated point, then turn back and knit in the other direction, a small hole will be created at the turning point. To avoid this hole, we use what is called a Wrap and Turn (W&T, see page 61).

Designing Your Own Socks
Once you learn the basics of sock knitting, you will probably want to design your own. Most of the sock knitting is straightforward;
however, the heel needs special attention. Keep the following general guidelines in mind when designing your own socks:
- Use half of the stitches on the knitting loom for the heel.
- Short-row down until $\frac{1}{3}$ of the pegs used for the heel are not W&T.
- For a narrower heel/wider heel—use fewer stitches or more stitches.
- The toe area is done exactly as the heel. At the end, close the toe by sewing.

Enjoy the magic of sock making!

Chunky Ribbed Socks

An easy introduction to socks—the stretchy ribs make it a perfect fit for almost every adult. Knitted with alpaca yarn for a most luxurious pair of socks.

You will need

Knitting Loom

Knitting loom with a peg multiple of 6
[Blue Knifty Knitter Loom was used in sample]

Yarn

150 yds. (137 m) of bulky yarn
[Ultra Alpaca Berroco 50% alpaca, 50% wool, 215 yds. (197 m) per 3.5 oz (100 g) ball used in sample]

Tools

Knitting tool
Tapestry needle

Size

Adult small

Gauge

9 st and 14 rows to 4 ins. (10 cm)

Pattern notes

K = Knit = Knit Stitch/Flat Panel
P = Purl
W&T = Wrap & Turn: Wrap:Take the loop off the peg, wrap the peg with the working yarn, re-place the loop back on the peg. Peg has 2 loops (leave with 2 loops). Turn: Knit back in the opposite direction.

Stitch Pattern

Round 1: P1, *k4, p2; rep from * to the last 5 sts, k4, p1.
Rep Rnd 1.

Work Sock Leg

Cast on in the round with cable cast-on method.

Round 1: P1, *k4, p2; rep from * to the last 5 sts, k4, p1.
Rep until leg measures 6 ins. (15 cm) from cast on edge.

Working the Short-row Heel

Note: The heel is worked as a flat panel. The cup for the heel is formed by knitting short rows. Remember to wrap each of the turning pegs.

Row 1: K11 (from peg 1–11), W&T peg 12.
Row 2: K10 (from peg 11–2), W&T peg 1.
Row 3: K9 (from peg 2–10), W&T peg 11.
Row 4: K8 (from peg 10–3), W&T peg 2.
Row 5: K7 (from peg 3–9), W&T peg 10.
Row 6: K6 (from peg 9–4), W&T peg 3.
Row 7: K5 (from peg 4–8), W&T peg 9.
Row 8: K4 (from peg 8–5), W&T peg 4.
Row 9: K5 (from peg 5–9) Make sure to knit 2 over 1 on peg 9.
Row 10: K6 (from peg 9–4) Make sure to knit 2 over 1 on peg 4.
Row 11: K7 (from peg 4–10) Be sure to knit 2 over 1 on peg 10.
Row 12: K8 (from peg 10–3) Be sure to knit 2 over 1 on peg 3.
Row 13: K9 (from peg 3–11). Knit 2 over 1 on peg 11.
Row 14: K10 (from peg 11–2). Knit 2 over 1 on peg 2.
Row 15: K11 (from peg 2–12) . Knit 2 over 1 on peg 12.
Row 16: K12 (from peg 12–1). Knit 2 over 1 on peg 1.

Working the Sock Foot

Note: The sock foot is worked in the round.
Round 1: K12, p1, k4, p2, k4, p1.
Next Rounds: Repeat rnd 1 until work measures 2 ins. (5 cm) less than desired length.

Shaping the Toe

Note: The toe is worked as a flat panel. The cup is formed by knitting short rows just like for the heel above. Remember to wrap each of the turning pegs.

Row 1: K11 (from peg 1–11),

W&T peg 12.
Row 2: K10 (from peg 11–2),
W&T peg 1.
Row 3: K9 (from peg 2–10),
W&T peg 11.
Row 4: K8 (from peg 10–3),
W&T peg 2.
Row 5: K7 (from peg 3–9),
W&T peg 10.
Row 6: K6 (from peg 9–4),
W&T peg 3.
Row 7: K5 (from peg 4–8),
W&T peg 9.
Row 8: K4 (from peg 8–5),
W&T peg 4.
Row 9: K5 (from peg 5–9). Make
sure to knit 2 over 1 on peg 9.
Row 10: K6 (from peg 9–4).
Knit 2 over 1 on peg 4.
Row 11: K7 (from peg 4–10).
Knit 2 over 1 on peg 10.
Row 12: K8 (from peg 10–3).
Knit 2 over 1 on peg 3.
Row 13: K9 (from peg 3–11).
Knit 2 over 1 on peg 11.
Row 14: K10 (from peg 11–2).
Knit 2 over 1 on peg 2.
Row 15: k11 (from peg 2–12).
Knit 2 over 1 on peg 12.
Row 16: k12 (from peg 12–1).
Knit 2 over 1 on peg 1.

Closing the Toe and Finishing
In preparation for closing the toe,
take the stitches off the knitting
loom and place them onto a pair
of size 8 (5 mm) knitting needles
like this: Take stitches from peg
1–12 and place them on 1
knitting needle. Take stitches
from peg 13–24 and place them
on the second knitting needle.

Graft the front and back stitches
together. Weave in all ends.
Block lightly.

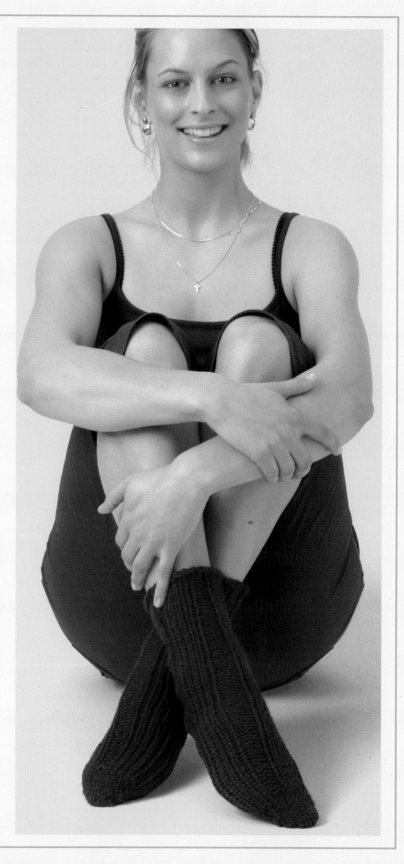

Circular Patterns

Now you have mastered the basic skills of loom knitting, here are some more patterns for you to try out. The following are all for a circular loom. Hopefully there will be something here to whet your appetite.

Mock Cables

Creating texture by twisting
stitches is easier than it looks

The principle of twisting stitches to create texture is fairly easy; it consists of two stitches interchanging places. No special tools are necessary. Every time stitches are crossed over one another, the knitted item shrinks horizontally, therefore twisting stitches makes the knitted piece narrower, than say knitting the same piece in stockinette stitch.

Most of the time, you will encounter twisted stitch patterns knitted on stockinette stitch on a background of reverse stockinette. The background of purl stitches helps bring out the twisted stitches and give them a three-dimensional appearance.

The crossed stitches presented in this section are two-stitch twist patterns. They work well as part of a rib stitch pattern, or as borders to give a flat panel extra dimension. There are two types of twists: right slanting and left slanting. They complement each other—if knitting a panel with a border at each side, you will place a right slanting cable on one side and the left slanting cable on the opposite side.

Let's get ready to do the twist—we will begin with the right slanting twist (TW or RTW) on a reverse stockinette background. We will assume that we are working on a knitting loom with 6 pegs, pegs will be numbered 1-6 (from right to left). Pegs 1 and 2 will be purled,

pegs 3 and 4 will be where the twist occurs, pegs 5 and 6 will be purled.

Classic Mock Cable instructions consist of the following 4 rows, as you can see the twist only happens in one row, row 3, the other rows are knitted normally.

Row 1, 2, 4: p2, k2, p2.
Row 3: p2, TW, p2.

How to twist the stitches for right slanting:

Take stitch from peg 3 off the knitting loom, hold it on your knitting tool, or on a cable needle, place it towards the center of the knitting loom. Move stitch from peg 4 to emptied peg 3. Place the

stitch from the cable needle on peg 4. Twist completed. After the twist is completed, knit the stitches as called for in the pattern.

How to twist the stitches for left slanting:

Take stitch from peg 4 off the knitting loom, hold it on your knitting tool, or on a cable needle, place it towards the center of the knitting loom. Move stitch from peg 3 to emptied peg 4. Place the stitch from the cable needle on peg 3. Twist completed. After the twist is completed, knit the stitches as called for in the pattern.

Row 1, 2, 4: p2, k2, p2.
Row 3: p2, LTW, p2.

Child's Mock Cable Hat

Learn the basics of crossing stitches while creating a classic hat. Choose some pretty colors and knit a hat in each one.

You will need

Knitting Loom

Large gauge child hat loom with a peg multiple of 4
[Round Green Knifty Knitter was used in sample]

Yarn

50 yards of bulky weight yarn
[GGH Aspen, 50% fine merino wool 50% Microfiber, 63 yds. (57 m) per 50g used in sample]

Tools

Knitting tool
Tapestry needle

Sizes

Child size

Gauge

8 stitches per inch

Pattern Notes

Knitted in the round.

TW: twist right (take the loops off pegs A & B, place stitch from peg A on peg B, place stitch from peg B on peg A). Knit them.

P2tog: A decrease row—combine the two purl stitches into one stitch by moving the stitch from the peg on the left to the peg on the right. (See Shaping section.)

Cable Twist Rib Pattern

multiple of 4 stitches:
Round 1, 2, 4: *P2, K2, repeat from *
Round 3: P2, TW

Stitch Pattern Chart

I	I	•	•	4
/	/	•	•	3
I	I	•	•	2
I	I	•	•	1
4	3	2	1	

Chart Key
K Knit I
P Purl •
TW Twist /

Body of Hat

Cast on in the round with the chain cast on method

Set up round: Purl to end.

Round 1, 2, 4: *P2, k2; rep from * to the end of round
Round 3: *P2, TW; rep from * to the end of round
Rep rounds 1–4, 7 times

Crown Shaping

*P2tog, k2; rep from * to the end of round (27 pegs with stitches).

Bind off with gathering method.

Children's Earflap Hats

The perfect child's hat—it will keep your little one's ears warm. Experiment with different color stripes, or different stitches to make different variations—perfect to show school or team spirit.

You will need

Knitting Loom

Large gauge child size hat loom [Round Green Knifty Knitter was used in sample]

Yarn

70 yds. of bulky weight yarn

- **Striped Version:** 50 yds. (46 m) Main Color, 20 yards (18 m) in secondary color [Rowan Big Wool (100% Merino wool, 87 yds (80 m) per 100 g in Bohemian and Black]

- **Solid Version:** 70 yds. (64 m) [Encore Mega Colorspun in color 7130 super bulky, 75% acrylic, 25% wool, 64 yds (59 m) per 100 g]

Tools

Knitting tool
Stitch holder
Tapestry needle

Gauge

5 sts and 8 rows to 2 ins. (5 cm)

Pattern notes

Knit = Knit Stitch
Main Color = MC
Contrasting Color = CC
When the pattern states, "using X color yarn", simply pick up the yarn color needed and start wrapping. Pattern is knit in the round, with the exception of the earflaps.
Solid Color Version: Use the same bulky color yarn throughout, omitting the color changes.

Earflap Instructions

Make 2
Knitted as Flat Panels in Garter Stitch.

Special Instructions

Decrease Row: K1, k2tog, knit to last 3 sts, ssk, k1.

Using CC cast on 8 stitches.
Row 1, 3, 5, 7: Purl.
Row 2, 4, 6: Knit.
Row 8: Decrease Row (6 sts left).
Row 9, 11, 13: Purl.
Row 10, 12: Knit.
Row 14: Decrease row (4 sts).
Row 15, 17: Purl.
Row 16: Knit.
Row 18: Decrease Row (2 sts).
Row 19: Purl.
Row 20 and on: Using the 2 stitches remaining on the loom knit a 2-stitch I-cord—15 ins. (38 cm) long.
Bind off. Weave in all yarn tail ends. Earflaps completed. Set aside.

Hat Body

Knitted in the round.
Cast on all pegs using MC and the chain cast-on method.

Hat Brim

Knitted in garter stitch as follows:
Row 1, 3, 5: Purl.
Row 2, 4, 6: Knit.
Attach CC at peg 1.

Attach Earflaps

Pick up 7 stitches from the earflaps' cast on edge and place them on the following pegs—on top of the loops already on the pegs:
Earflap 1: Place on pegs 1–7.
Earflap 2: Place on pegs 19–25.

Continue knitting body of the hat:
Row 7–8: Using CC knit 2 rows.
On Row 7, make sure to knit 2 over 1 on pegs 1–7, and 19–25.
Cut CC.
Row 9–20: Using MC: Knit 12 rows.
Row 21–23: Attach CC: Knit 3 rows with CC.
Row 24: Knit 1 row in MC.
Row 25–27: Knit 3 rows in CC.
Row 28–30: Knit 3 rows in MC.

(continued on next page)

 TIP

To decrease the crown of the hat, knit it in flat panels. Divide the number of the pegs used into wedges that contain the same number of stitches. Work each wedge as a flat panel and decrease each flat panel to make a triangle. At the end, seam the wedges with an invisible seam like the mattress stitch.

Crown of Hat

The crown of the hat is knit in four wedges of nine stitches each and later seamed together.

Special Instructions:
Decrease Row: K1, k2tog, knit to last 3 sts, ssk, k1.

Knit wedges as follows:
Row 1, 3, 5, 7, 9: Knit.
Row 2, 4, 6, 8: Decrease row—follow special instructions above. Place the last stitch on a stitch holder. Cut yarn and attach the yarn to the next wedge.

Wedge 1 (pegs 1–9).
Wedge 2 (pegs 10–18).
Wedge 3 (pegs 19–27).
Wedge 4 (pegs 28–36).
Seam the wedges together using mattress stitch.

Place the 4 stitches from the stitch holder back onto the knitting loom, 2 stitches on peg 1 and 2 stitches on peg 2.
Knit a 6–inch, 2 stitch I-cord. Bind off the I-cord and form a small knot with the I-cord to make a bobble.

Turn hat inside out and weave in all the yarn ends, making sure to cross the yarns where the color changes occurred to prevent any holes.

Cowl

The cowl is knitted with brushed alpaca yarn for a soft neck covering to keep out the chills. You can wear this cowl two ways—around your neck, or over the head—but whichever way you choose, wear it with style.

You will need

Knitting Loom

Large gauge knitting loom with at least 40 pegs
[Yellow Knifty Knitter was used in sample]

Yarn

110 yds. (101 m) of baby alpaca yarn
[Plymouth Baby Alpaca Brush, 80% Baby Alpaca, 20% Acrylic, 110 yds (101 m) per 50g used in sample]

Tools

Knitting tool
Tapestry needle

Size

14 ins. W x 22 ins. L
(36 cm x 56 cm)

Gauge

13 sts and 14 rows to
4 ins. (10 cm)

Pattern notes

Knitted as a flat panel.
Sl = Skip the stitch with yarn in the back
K = knit=knit stitch/flat stitch
p = purl

Instructions

Cast on 40 sts with crochet chain method.
Row 1: Sl1, k to the end.
Row 2: Sl1, p2, k to last 3 sts, p3.

Repeat rows 1 and 2 until item measures 22 inches (56 cm) from cast on edge.

Bind off with basic bind-off method.

Assembly

Seam the cast-on edge to the bind off edge.
Block lightly.
Wear with panache.

Ribbed Leg Warmers

These leg warmers are cozy and comfortable to wear. Knitted completely in rib stitch to provide a stretchy fit. Wear them under skirts to keep your legs warm, over your jeans for a retro look, or under your jeans and allow only a few inches to show below your jeans.

You will need

Knitting Loom

24 Peg large gauge knitting loom [Round Blue Knifty Knitter was used in sample]

Yarn

Approximately 180 yards (165 m) of bulky weight wool [2 balls of Crystal Palace Iceland, 100% Wool, 109 yds (99 m) per 100 gram ball, was used in sample, color 7256]

Tools

Knitting tool
Tapestry needle

Size

22 ins. (56 cm) Long

Gauge

6 stitches and 8 rows to 2 ins. (5 cm) over rib stitch

Pattern notes

Knitted in the round using all the pegs on the knitting loom.
Knit: refers to the knit stitch/ flat stitch.

Stitch Pattern

K2, P2, repeat from * to * to the end of the round.

Instructions

(Make 2)
Cast on with the e-wrap cast-on method.

Round 1: *K2, P2*, repeat from * to * to the end of the round. Continue in pattern until item measures 22 ins. (56 cm) from cast-on edge.

Bind off using the single crochet bind off method.

 TIP

The cast on and bind off need to be done loosely or they will be tight around the legs.

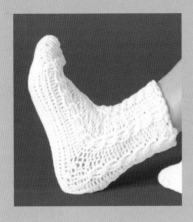

Sock Patterns

Knitting socks is my favorite pastime. Once you get the knack you'll be designing your own. Until then try out these two mock-cable patterns, one fine and one chunkier, to get you on the path.

Mock Cable Socks

Socks that you can wear with everyday shoes are possible to loom knit; all you need is a loom that will give you the gauge desired. In this pattern, we used a knitting loom that will provide you with a pair of socks that you can wear with your everyday shoes. The pattern is knitted with a modified mock cable.

You will need

Knitting Loom

Extra fine gauge sock loom with a peg multiple of 4 [Decor Accents extra fine gauge knitting loom used]

Yarn

200 yards of fingering weight/sock weight yarn. [Koigu Premium Merino, 100% merino wool, 175 yds. (160 m) per 50 g, was used in sample]

Tools

Knitting tool
Tapestry needle
2 size 2 (2.75 mm)
Double pointed needles (dpns)

Size

Small women's size

Gauge

8 stitches per inch
(2.5 cm)

Pattern notes

Knitted in the round.

RTW: Twist right (take the loops off pegs A and B, place stitch from peg A on peg B, place stitch from peg B on peg A). Knit them.

Cable Twist Rib Pattern

Multiple of 4
Round 1, 2, 4: K1, P1, K2
Round 3: K1, P1, TW

Stitch Pattern Chart

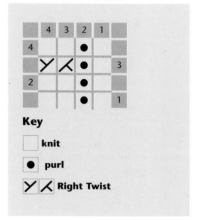

Key

□ knit

● purl

Ⲩⲕ Right Twist

Sock Leg

Note: Rounds 1–4 are the Cable Twist Rib pattern, a 4-stitch repeat.

Cast on in the round with chain cast on method.

Round 1, 2, 4: K1, P1, K2

Round 3: K1, P1, RTW

Repeat rounds 1–4 (Cable Twist Rib pattern) until item measures 6.5 ins. (16.5 cm) from cast-on edge (or desired length).

End sock leg with a round 4 in preparation for short-row heel.

Working the Short-row heel

Note: The heel is worked as a flat panel. The cup for the heel is formed by knitting short rows. Remember to wrap each of the turning pegs.

Knit heel as instructed in the short-row heel chart (right).

Working the Sock Foot

Note: Knit the sole and instep areas of the sock in the round. Instep area will have mock cables, sole of foot will be in stockinette stitch.

**Rnd 1, 2, 4: K34, [K1, P1, K2] 8 times, end with K2.

Rnd 3: K34, [K1, P1, RTW] 8 times, end with RTW**.

(Rounds 1–4: Knit 34, from peg 35–68 follow Mock Cable Stitch pattern instructions).

Next Rounds: Repeat from ** to ** until 2 ins. (5 cm) less than desired length.

Shaping the Toe

Note: The toe is worked as a flat panel. The cup is formed by knitting short-rows as in the heel. Remember to wrap each of the turning pegs.

Short Row Heel Chart

68 Peg Loom – 10ins. (25.5cm)

Part I: Decrease		Part II: Increase	
Knit from Peg to Peg	Wrap peg. These pegs will have 2 loops on them. Lift the loop on the peg, wrap the peg, place loop back on the peg.	Be sure to knit over 2 over 1 on the pegs with the extra loop on them.	
■ 1-34	35	■ 13-24
■ 34-2	1	■ 24-12
■ 2-33	34	■ 12-25
■ 33-3	2	■ 25-11
■ 3-32	33	■ 11-26
■ 32-4	3	■ 26-10
■ 4-31	32	■ 10-27
■ 31-5	4	■ 27-9
■ 5-30	31	■ 9-28
■ 30-6	5	■ 28-8
■ 6-29	30	■ 8-29
■ 29-7	6	■ 29-7
■ 7-28	29	■ 7-30
■ 28-8	7	■ 30-6
■ 8-27	28	■ 6-31
■ 27-9	8	■ 31-5
■ 9-26	27	■ 5-32
■ 26-10	9	■ 32-4
■ 10-25	26	■ 4-33
■ 25-11	10	■ 33-3
■ 11-24	25	■ 3-34
■ 24-12	11	■ 34-2
■ 12-23	24	■ 2-35
■ 23-13	12	■ 35-1

Repeat short row heel chart.

Closing the Toe

In preparation for closing the toe, take the stitches off the knitting loom and place them onto 2, size 1 or 2 (2.25 mm or 2.75 mm) knitting needles.

Take stitches from pegs 1–32 and place them on one needle. Take stitches from pegs 32–64 and place them on the second knitting needle.

Graft front and back stitches together using the Kitchener stitch.

Weave in all ends.
Block lightly.

Weekend Socks

Spend your weekend morning lounging around in style. The Weekend Socks sport the classic mock cables with a background of reverse stockinette.

You will need

Knitting Loom

Large gauge sock size knitting loom. Blue (24 peg) Knifty Knitter was used in sample.

Yarn

200–250 yds. (183–229 m) bulky weight yarn [GGH Aspen (50% Fine Merino Wool, 50% Microfiber, 63 yds (58 m) per 50g used in sample]

Tools

Knitting tool
Tapestry needle
Pair size 8 (5 mm) knitting needles for grafting

Measurements

Women's small to medium

Gauge

10 stitches and 15 rows to 4 ins. (10 cm)

Pattern notes

Knitted in the round
TW = Twist
Twist right (take the loops off pegs A and B, place stitch from A on peg B, place stitch from peg B on peg A). Knit the two stitches.

W&T = Wrap & Turn:
Wrap: Take the loop off the peg, wrap the peg with the working yarn, re-place the loop back on the peg. Peg has 2 loops.
Turn: Knit back in the opposite direction.

Note

Adjust the suggested size by knitting more or fewer rounds in the leg and foot area.

Stitch Pattern

Mock Cable Rib Pattern: 4-stitch repeat
Round 1, 2, 4: [p1, k2, p1] 6 times
Round 3: [p1, TW, p1] 6 times

Chart

•				•	4
•	/		/	•	3
•				•	2
•				•	1
4	3		2	1	

Chart Key
K Knit |
P Purl •
TW Twist /

WORK SOCK LEG

Cast on 24 stitches with chain cast on in the round.
Note: Rounds 1–4 are the mock cable rib pattern

Round 1, 2, 4: [P1, k2, p1] 6 times.
Round 3: [P1, TW, p1] 6 times.

Repeat Rounds 1–4 (mock cable rib pattern) until leg measures 6 ins. (15 cm) from cast-on edge or 7 Mock Cable Rib Pattern repetitions have been completed.
End sock leg with round 4.

Working Short-row Heel

Note: The heel is worked as a flat panel. The cup for the heel is formed by knitting short rows. Remember to wrap each of the turning pegs.

Row 1: K11 (from peg 1–11), W&T peg 12.
Row 2: K10 (from peg 11–2), W&T peg 1.
Row 3: K9 (from peg 2–10), W&T peg 11.
Row 4: K8 (from peg 10–3), W&T peg 2.
Row 5: K7 (from peg 3–9), W&T peg 10.
Row 6: K6 (from peg 9–4), W&T peg 3.
Row 7: K5 (from peg 4–8), W&T peg 9.
Row 8: K4 (from peg 8–5), W&T peg 4.

(continued on next page)

Row 9: K5 (from peg 5–9). Make sure to knit 2 over 1 on peg 9.
Row 10: K6 (from peg 9–4). Make sure to knit 2 over 1 on peg 4.
Row 11: K7 (from peg 4–10). Be sure to knit 2 over 1 on peg 10.
Row 12: K8 (from peg 10–3). Be sure to knit 2 over 1 on peg 3.
Row 13: K9 (from peg 3–11). Be sure to knit 2 over 1 on peg 11.
Row 14: K10 (from peg 11–2). Be sure to knit 2 over 1 on peg 2.
Row 15: K11 (from peg 2–12). Be sure to knit 2 over 1 on peg 12.
Row 16: K12 (from peg 12–1) Make sure to knit 2 over 1 on peg 1.

Working the Sock Foot

Note: The sock foot is worked in the round.

Rounds 1, 2, 4: k12, [p1, k2, p1] 3 times.
Round 3: k12, [p1, TW, p1] 3 times.

Next Rounds: repeat rounds 1–4 until 2 ins. (5 cm) less than desired length.

SHAPING THE TOE

Note: The toe is worked as a flat panel. The cup is formed by knitting short rows just like above for the heel. Remember to wrap each of the turning pegs.

Row 1: K11 (from peg 1–11), W&T peg 12.
Row 2: K10 (from peg 11–2), W&T peg 1.
Row 3: K9 (from peg 2–10), W&T peg 11.

Row 4: K8 (from peg 10–3), W&T peg 2.
Row 5: K7 (from peg 3–9), W&T peg 10.
Row 6: K6 (from peg 9–4), W&T peg 3.
Row 7: K5 (from peg 4–8), W&T peg 9.
Row 8: K4 (from peg 8–5), W&T peg 4.
Row 9: K5 (from peg 5–9). Make sure to knit 2 over 1 on peg 9.
Row 10: K6 (from peg 9–4). Make sure to knit 2 over 1 on peg 4.
Row 11: K7 (from peg 4–10). Be sure to knit 2 over 1 on peg 10.
Row 12: K8 (from peg 10–3). Be sure to knit 2 over 1 on peg 3.
Row 13: K9 (from peg 3–11). Be sure to knit 2 over 1 on peg 11.
Row 14: K10 (from peg 11–2). Knit 2 over 1 on peg 2.

Row 15: K11 (from peg 2–12). Knit 2 over 1 on peg 12.
Row 16: K12 (from peg 12–1). Knit 2 over 1 on peg 1.

Closing the toe and finishing

In preparation for closing the toe, take the stitches off the knitting loom and place them onto two, size 8 (5 mm) knitting needles.

Take stitches from peg 1–12 and place them on one knitting needle. Take stitches from peg 13–24 and place them on the second knitting needle.

Graft front and back stitches together using the Kitchener stitch. Weave in all ends.
Block lightly.

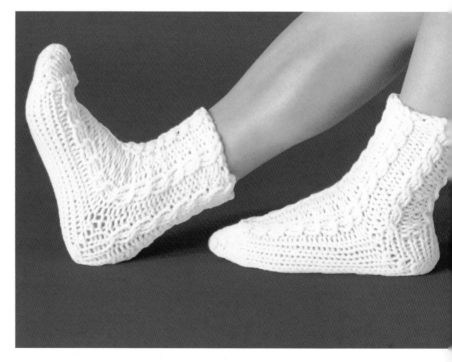

Flat Panel Patterns

These are all knitted in flat panels or single rakes. This doesn't meant you need a special loom, you can knit these on a circular loom just by not joining them up into a round. Have fun!

Brocade Baby Sweater

This baby sweater has a simple drop-shoulder and boatneck design. It is knitted with a non-itchy wool blend yarn that does not shed making this yarn great for baby projects.

You will need

Knitting Loom

Large gauge knitting loom with at least 23 (27, 31) pegs. Green Knifty Knitter was used in sample.

Yarn

160 (180, 220) yards (146, 165, 201 m) of bulky weight yarn [GGH Aspen, 50% fine merino wool, 50% Microfiber, 63 yds. (58 m) per 50g, was used in sample]

Other

2 buttons

Tools

Knitting tool
Tapestry needle

Size

newborn (6 months, 12 months)

Gauge

10 sts and 16 rows to 4 ins. (10 cm)

Pattern notes

Knitted as 4 flat panels
K = knit = knit stitch
P = purl
stockinette stitch = knit every row
st(s) = stitch(es)
mk1 = make 1 with the Lifted Increase method (see page 59)
BO = bind off
The instructions will be presented as follows: newborn (6 months, 12 months). Where only one number appears, follow the same instructions apply for all sizes.
Note: the first and last stitch are selvedge stitches. Always knit the first stitch and knit the last stitch in the row. They are not part of the stitch pattern.

Stitch Pattern

Mini Brocade Stitch
Multiple of 4+1 over 5 rows

5	4	3	2	1	
		•			5
	•		•		4
•				•	3
	•		•		2
		•			1

Key

□ **knit** knit stitch
● **purl** purl stitch

Pattern:
R1 (RS): k2, p, k2
R2: k, p, k, p, k
R3: p, k3, p
R4: k, p, k, p, k
R5: k2, p, k2

Back

Cast on 23 (27, 31) sts with crochet chain method.

Hemline

All sizes
Row 1, 3: K to the end.
Row 2, 4: P to the end. Small sizes stop. 12 months continue.
Row 5: K to the end.
Row 6: P to the end.
Next: All sizes knit 2 rows in stockinette stitch.

Mini Brocade Stitch Pattern

Row 1: K3, *p1, k3; rep from * to end.
Row 2: K2, *p1, k1; repeat from * to last 2 sts, k2.
Row 3: K1, p1, *k3, p1; rep from * to last st, k1.
Row 4: K2, p1, *k1, p1; rep from * to last 2 sts, k2.

Rep Rows 1–4: 8 (9, 10) more times, ending on a row 1.

Neckline

Knit 2 rows.
Bind off with basic removal method.

Front

Follow instructions for back, stopping at neckline instructions.

Front Neckline

Next row: k6, BO9, k6 (k8, BO11, k8 • k9, BO13, k9).

Divide neckline into two parts. Each part has 6 (8, 9) pegs.
Next row: K6 (k8, k9). **Next row:** k6 (k8, k9).

Make Buttonholes
Next row: K1 (k1, k2), k2tog, k1 (k2, k1), k2tog (k1, k2).
Next row: K2 (k2, k3), co1, k1 (k2, k1), co1, k1 (k2, k3).
Next row: K6 (k8, k9). Bind off. Join yarn to the other side.
Next row: K6 (k8, k9). Bind off.

Sleeves
(Make 2)
Cast on 15 (19, 23) sts with crochet chain method.

Cuff
All sizes
Row 1, 3: K to the end.
Row 2, 4: P to the end.
Small sizes stop—12 months continue:
Row 5: K to the end.
Row 6: P to the end.
All sizes:
Next row: Knit.
Next row: K2, mk1, k to last 2 sts, mk1, k2. 17 (21, 23) sts total.
Next row: *K3, p1; rep from * to the last st, p1.
Next row: K1, M1, p1, *k1, p1; rep from * to last st, M1, k1. 19 (23, 27) sts total.
Next row: K1, p1, *k3, p1; rep from * to last st, k1.
Next row: K2, p1, *k1, p1; rep from * to last 2 sts, k2.
Continue in mini brocade pattern.
Row 1: K3, *p1, k3; rep from * to end.
Row 2: K2, *p1, k1; repeat from * to last 2 sts, k2.
Row 3: K1, p1, *k3, p1; rep from * to last st, k1.
Row 4: K2, p1, *k1, p1; rep from * to last 2 sts, k2.
Repeat mini brocade pattern: 5 (6, 7) more times. Total repetitions: 7 (8, 9).

Next row: Knit Row 1.
Next row: Knit.
Bind off. Block lightly.
Weave in all ends.

Assembly
Seam all sides. **Note:** leave the front side where the buttonholes are located un-seamed.
Attach 2 buttons to the back neckline to correspond with the buttonholes.

Newborn

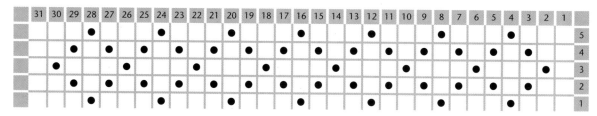

6 months

12 months

Key
☐ **knit** knit stitch
● **purl** purl stitch

Garter Stitch Scarf

One simple design can be used for a quick thin fashionable scarf, or wider for a warm wrap. We knitted the thin style in the red yarn to match the garter stitch hat and fingerless gloves. For added pizazz, add some long tassels or a fringe.

You will need

Knitting Loom

Large gauge knitting loom with 12 (40) pegs
[Round Yellow Knifty Knitter was used in sample]

Yarn

Thin Scarf: 160 yds. (146 m) super bulky weight yarn [Rowan Big Wool, 100% wool, 87 yds. (79 m) per 100 g, in Bohemian]
Wide Scarf: 360 yds. (329 m) bulky weight yarn [Patons Glittallic, 360 yds. (329 m) in Lilac and Lion Brand Jiffy 360 yds. (329 m) in Pearl Gray—Use 2 strands as 1 thru'out pattern] (See p142 for picture)

Tools

Knitting Tool

Size

72 ins. x 6 ins. (183 cm x 15 cm) / 8 ins. (20.5 cm)

Gauge

8 stitches and 12 rows to 4 ins. (10 cm)

Pattern notes
Knitted as a flat panel
Slip the first stitch at the beginning of each row
Knit = Knit Stitch throughout

Stitch Pattern: Garter Stitch

Note: The scarves were knitted with the Knit Stitch. If you desire a more open weave, I recommend knitting with the single stitch instead.

Instructions
Cast on 12 (40) stitches.

Row 1: Slip 1, purl 10 (38), K1.
Row 2: Slip 1, knit to the end of the row.
Repeat Rows 1 and 2 until scarf

TIP

When adding another skein of yarn, add it at the beginning of a row. Make sure to leave at least a 5-inch (12.5 cm) tail at the end of the old skein and on the beginning of the new skein. For a nice chain edge, slip the first stitch and knit the last stitch of each row.

measures 72 ins. (183 cm) or desired length.

Bind off using the flat removal method.

Optional: Add fringes. Weave in yarn ends.

Velvety Soft Blanket and Hat

The name of the blanket and hat describes it perfectly. The yarn used for the project is next to the skin worthy—perfect for a newborn baby. Knitted with a large gauge knitting loom this baby layette knits fast.

You will need

Knitting Loom

For Blanket: 40 peg large gauge knitting loom [Yellow Knifty Knitter was used in sample]

For Hat: Large gauge newborn size hat loom or large gauge baby size hat loom [Blue Knifty Knitter was used for the sample]

Yarn

For Blanket: 165 yds. (150 m) of bulky weight chenille yarn [3 skeins of Lion Brand Velvetspun, 100% Polyester, 54 yds (49 m) per 3 oz. (85 g) used in sample: 2 Carnation, 1 White.

For Hat: 50 yards of bulky weight chenille Yarn [Lion Brand Velvetspun, 100% Polyester, 54 yds. (49 m) per 3 oz. (85 g) was used in sample]

Tools

Knitting Tool
Tapestry Needle

Size

Blanket: 22 ins. x 22 ins. (56 cm)
Hat: Newborn – 6 months

Gauge

For Blanket: 3.5 stitches and 7.5 rows to 2 ins. (5 cm)
For Hat: 3.5 stitches and 7.5 rows to 2 ins. (5 cm)

Pattern notes (Blanket)

Knitted as a flat panel.
Main Color (MC) Carnation.
Contrasting Color (CC) White.
ss = single stitch.

Stitch Pattern:

Garter Stitch
Row 1: slip 1, purl 38, ss1.
Row 2: slip 1, ss to end.

Instructions

With MC, Cast on for 40 pegs with the chain cast on method.
Work in garter stitch for 26 rows. Cut MC leaving a 5 ins. (12.5 cm) tail. Join CC leaving a 5 ins. (12.5 cm) beginning tail.
Work in garter stitch for another 26 rows. Cut CC leaving a 5 ins. (12.5 cm) tail. Attach MC leaving a 5 ins. (12.5 cm) beginning tail.
Work garter stitch pattern for 26 rows.

Bind off.
Weave in all yarn tail ends.

Pattern notes (Hat)

Knitted in the round.
Main color (MC) Carnation.
Contrasting color (CC) White.
Knitted in single stitch

Instructions

Using CC cast on in the round with chain cast on method.

Hat brim

Row 1: purl
Row 2: knit in single stitch
Row 3: purl. Cut CC, leaving a 5-ins. (12.5-cm) tail.
Row 4: join MC. Knit in single stitch.

Continue knitting in single stitch until item measures 5 ins–6 ins. (12.5 cm–15 cm) from cast on edge.
Bind off using gather removal method. Weave in yarn ends.

Tip: Wrap loosely when knitting with chenille yarn. It breaks very easily! Be sure to bind in the ends well so it doesn't unravel.

TIP

For a nice chain edge, slip the first stitch and knit the last stitch of each row.

Bliss Baby Blanket

This baby blanket is knitted in Debbie Bliss Cashmerino, an exquisitely soft, washable yarn. The yarn is gentle on the skin and it knits up fast on a large gauge knitting loom.

You will need

Knitting Loom

Large gauge knitting loom [Yellow Knifty Knitter was used in sample]

Yarn

950 yds. (868 m) of bulky weight yarn [Debbie Bliss Cashmerino Super Chunky, 55% merino wool, 33% microfibre, 12% cashmere, 83 yds. (76 m) per 100 g, was used in sample]

Tools

Knitting tool
Tapestry needle
Crochet hook

Size

36 ins. x 38 ins.
(91 cm x 97 cm)

Gauge

12 sts and 20 rows to 4 ins. (10 cm) in stockinette stitch
Make sure you check gauge

Pattern notes

Knitted as 3 flat panels
K = Knit = Knit Stitch/Flat Stitch
P = Purl
Rep = Repeat

Stitch Patterns

Moss Stitch
Row 1: *P1, k1; rep from * to the end of row. Rep.

Stockinette Stitch
Knit every row in Knit Stitch

Tip: To make the finishing easier, try to attach the yarn on the same side of the panel each time.

Panel 1 (Make 1)
Cast on 38 stitches with chain cast on method. The first and last stitches are selvedge stitches.

**Row 1: K1, (p1, k1) 18 times, k1
Rep row 1 until panel measures 12 ins. (30 cm) **.
Next Rows: Knit in stockinette stitch for 12 ins. (30 cm).
Repeat from ** to **.
Bind off with basic removal method.

Panel 2 (Make 2)
Cast on 38 stitches with chain cast on method.
The first and last stitches are selvedge stitches.
Row 1: K1, (p1, k1) 18 times, k1
Rep Row 1 until panel measures 38 ins. (97 cm).

Bind off with basic removal method.

Assembly

Block the pieces lightly prior to assembly.
Place first panel knitted in the middle of the other two panels (see assembly diagram below).
Use mattress stitch to seam the panels. Weave in all ends.
Once all the panels are assembled, single crochet all around the blanket to neaten the edges.

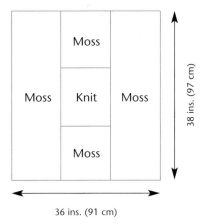

36 ins. (91 cm)

38 ins. (97 cm)

Mock Cables Poncho

Ponchos are a classic garment—perfect for young people who need to keep warm, while remaining stylish at all times of course. An easy knit and versatile item of clothing, this poncho is knitted with a large gauge knitting loom and bulky yarn to grow quickly.

You will need

Knitting Loom

Large gauge knitting loom with a peg number multiple of 8 + 2

Yarn

256 (315, 441) yds. [232, 290, 406 m] of bulky weight wool [GGH Aspen in Off White (50% fine merino wool, 50% microfiber, 63 yds. (58 m) per 50g, used in sample]

Tools

Knitting tool
Tapestry needle

Sizes

Children 4 (6, 8) years
(middle size shown)
See the poncho conversion chart at back of book for other sizes

Gauge

6 stitches and 8 rows to 2 ins. (5 cm) when blocked

Pattern notes

Knitted as flat panels
Knit stands for Knit Stitch/Flat Stitch
First and last stitches are selvedge stitches. Always knit them.

Stitch Pattern — Mock Cable

TW = Twist
1 Twist right (take the loops off pegs A and B, place stitch from A on peg B, place stitch from peg B on peg A).
2 Knit the two stitches.

Stitch Pattern Chart

•	•	|	|	•	•	|	|	4
•	•	/	/	•	•	|	|	3
•	•	|	|	•	•	|	|	2
•	•	|	|	•	•	|	|	1
8	7	6	5	4	3	2	1	

Chart Key
K Knit |
P Purl •
TW Twist /

Panels (Make 2)

Note: The first and last stitch are selvedge stitches, they are not part of the stitch pattern.
Rows 1–4 are the mock cable stitch pattern, an 8-stitch repeat.

Cast on 22 (28, 36) stitches with chain cast on method.

Row 1, 2, 4: Slip 1, [k2, p2, k2, p2] 2, (3), 4 times, K3.
Row 3: Slip 1, [k2, p2, TW, p2] 2, (3), 4 times, k3.

Work until panel measures 18 (21, 25 ins.) [46, 53, 64 cm] or you have repeated rows 1–4, 18 (21) 25 times.

End by working a row 4.

Bind Off

Remove with basic flat panel removal method.

Block pieces to the following measurements:
10 x 21 ins. (12 x 24 ins., 14 x 29 ins.) or 25.5 cm (30 x 61 cm, 36 x 74 cm).

Assembly

Assemble the poncho by seaming a long side to a short side. Fold over into poncho shape and seam a short side to a long side. See assembly diagram below.

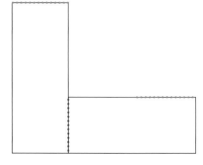

Fingerless Mitts

These easy hand warmers can keep your hands toasty while allowing finger movement—perfect for those early mornings at the computer or knitting on a cold day. Knit them to match the cosy garter stitch hat and scarf.

You will need

Knitting Loom

Large gauge knitting loom [Round Green Knifty Knitter used in sample]

Yarn

50 yards (46 m) super bulky weight yarn [Rowan Big Wool, 100% wool, 87 yds. (79 m) per 100 g, in Bohemian, used in sample]

Tools

Knitting Tool
Tapestry needle
Stitch marker

Size

Adult

Gauge

8 stitches and 12 rows to 4 ins. (10 cm) over garter stitch

Pattern notes

Knitted as a flat panel
Knit refers to the knit stitch/ flat stitch

Instructions

Make 2.
Cast on 18 stitches with the chain cast on method, leaving a beginning yarn tail of about 20 ins. (51 cm).
Row 1 and 3: Purl to the end.
Row 2 and 4: Knit to the end.
Row 5–14: Knit to the end.
Row 15: Increase 1 stitch at beginning of row. Knit 18 sts.
Row 16: Increase 1 stitch at beginning of row. Knit 19 sts.

2 Stitches were increased in rows 15 and 16. Twenty stitches are now on the knitting loom.
Row 17–26: Knit to the end.

Row 27: Purl to the end (place an open ring stitch marker on the third stitch of this row).
Row 28: Knit to the end.
Row 29: Purl to the end.
Bind off loosely using flat removal method 1, leaving a 10 ins. (25.5 cm) yarn tail.

Assembly

Using the yarn tail end from the cast-on edge and mattress stitch, seam the side of the mitt. Stop 1.5 ins. (4 cm) from the row with the stitch marker. Cut yarn. Thread the tapestry needle through the yarn tail end on the bind-off edge. Use mattress stitch to seam the side, stopping when you reach the row with the stitch marker. Weave the yarn ends into the wrong side of the item. Remove all stitch markers.

Eyeglasses Case

This is a great project to try out a new stitch pattern. Here we have used double moss, or seed stitch, but any will do.

You will need

Knitting Loom

Large gauge loom with 18 pegs [Round Blue Knifty Knitter used in sample]

Yarn

 40 yards (37 m) of bulky weight yarn [Simply Soft Quick, 100% Acrylic, 50 yds. (46 m) per 3 oz. used in sample]

Tools

Knitting tool
Tapestry needle

Size

5.5 ins. x 3 ins.
(14 cm x 7.5 cm)

Gauge

6 stitches and 10 rows to 2 inches (5 cm) over double moss stitch

Assembly diagram

Fold along this line

Pattern notes

Knitted as a flat panel

Stitch Pattern

Double Moss Stitch: Multiple of 2 stitches.
Row 1: *K1, P1, repeat from * to the end of the row.
Row 2: *P1, K1, repeat from * to the end of the row.
Row 3: *P1, K1, repeat from * to the end of the row.
Row 4: *K1, P1, repeat from * to the end of the row.

Instructions

Cast on with the crochet chain method on 18 pegs.
Knit in double moss stitch pattern until item measures 6.5 ins. (16.5 cm) from CO edge.

Bind off 2 stitches. Knit 14. Bind off last 2 stitches. Cut yarn.

Attach yarn to the fourteenth stitch. Continue knitting in double moss stitch pattern for 1.5 ins. (4 cm).
Next row: Continue knitting in pattern as follows: Knit first 3 stitches in pattern. K2Tog. Knit in pattern to the last four stitches. K2Tog. Knit in stitch pattern to the end.
Next row: Continue knitting in pattern. Remember to cast on a stitch on the fourth peg. Continue in pattern for another 1 inch (2.5 cm). Bind off with the basic bind off method.

Assembly

Fold the eyeglasses case in half. Mattress stitch the short side seams. Attach two buttons so they match the buttonhole openings made by the K2tog.
Weave in all yarn ends.

Ruana

Cozy, elegant, this Ruana will provide you with warmth during those fall days. It can be worn in different styles: let the front and back down or throw one of the front panels up around your shoulders for a sophisticated look, or place both front panels around the shoulders.

You will need

Knitting Loom

Large gauge knitting loom with at least 40 pegs
[Yellow Knifty Knitter used in sample]

Yarn

1066 yards (974 m) of bulky weight yarn
[13 balls of Debbie Bliss Cashmerino super chunky, 12% cashmere, 55% merino wool, 33% microfiber, 71 yds. (65 m) per 50gm, was used in sample]

Tools

Knitting tool
Stitch markers

Size

30 ins. (76 cm) wide
x 56 ins. (142 cm) long

Gauge

12 stitches and 20 rows to 4 ins. (10 cm) in stockinette stitch

Pattern notes

K: knit=knit stitch/flat stitch
P: purl
RTW: twist right (take the loops off pegs A & B, place stitch from peg A on peg B, place stitch from peg B on peg A)
LTW: twist left, mirror image of RTW
Note: Knitted in two panels.

Border Edge Patterns

Mock Cable outside edge stitch pattern completed over 6 stitches
Left Side Panel
Row 1, 2, 3: p2, K2, p2.
Row 4: p2, RTW, p1.
Repeat Rows 1–4.

Chart 1: Mock Cable Edge

Legend:

☐ knit

● purl

⟍⟋ Right Twist

Notes:
Pattern:
R1 (RS): p2, k2, p2
R2: p2, k2, p2
R3: p2, k2, p2
R4: p2, Right Twist, p2

Moss Stitch inside edge stitch pattern — completed over 4 stitches.
Row 1: *k1, p1; rep from * to end.
Row 2: rep row 1.
Repeat Rows 1 and 2.

Chart 2: Moss Stitch

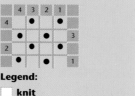

Legend:

☐ knit

● purl

Part I Left side Panel:

See chart 3: Left Side Panel

Set up: Place stitch markers on pegs 3 and 4 to mark the mock cable stitches. Place the remaining 4 stitch markers on the last 4 pegs (pegs 37–40).
Cast on 40 sts using chain method.

Row 1, 3: P2, k2, p2, k30, (k1, p1) 2 times.
Row 2: (K, p) 2 times, k30, p2, k2, p2.
Row 4: (K, p) 2 times, k30, p2, RTW, p2.
Rep rows 1–4, 25 times (25 cables).

Shaping the neckline (over 20 rows): the moss stitch is extended over 10 more stitches. The outside edge maintains the mock cable stitch edge. (See Chart 5).
Row 1, 3, 5: P2, k2, p2, k20, (k1, p1) 7 times.
Row 2: (K, p) 7 times, k20, p2, k2, p2.
Row 4: (K, p) 7 times, k20, p2, RTW, p2.

Neckline opening

Row 6: BO 10, (k,p) 2 times, k20, p2, k2, k2 (30 stitches remain on loom).

Row 7: P2, k2, p2, k20, (k1, p1) 2 times.

Row 8: (K, p) 2 times, k20, p2, RTW, p2.

Row 9: P2, k2, p2, k20, (k1, p1) 2 times.

Row 10: (K, p) 2 times, k20, p2, k2, p2.

Row 11: Rep row 9.

Row 12: Rep row 8.

Row 13: Rep row 9.

Row 14: CO 10 sts, rep row 10.

Row 15: K2, p2, k2, k20, (k1, p1), 7 times.

Row 16: (K, p) 7 times, k20, p2, RTW, p2.

Row 17: Rep Row 15.

Row 18: (K, p) 7 times, k20, p2, k2, p2.

Row 19: Rep row 15.

Row 20: Rep row 16.

End of Neckline shaping.

**Next row: P2, k2, p2, k34.

Next row: K34, p2, k2, p2.

Next row: P2, k2, p2, k34.

Next row: K34, p2, RTW, p2**.

Rep from ** to ** 24 more times (you should have 25 mock cables). Knit 6 rows of Moss stitch. (Moss Stitch: *K, p; rep from * to the end of row). Bind off with basic removal method.

Part II Right Side Panel:

(See chart 4: Right side panel) Place stitch markers on pegs 37 and 38 to mark the mock cable stitches. Place the remaining 4 stitch markers on the first 4 pegs (pegs 1–4).

Cast on 40 stitches using chain cast on method.

Row 1, 3: (P1, k1) 2 times, k30, p2, k2, p2.

Row 2: P2, k2, p2, k30, (p1, k1) 2 times.

Row 4: P2, LTW, p2, k30, (p1, k1) 2 times.

Rep rows 1–4 24 more times—25 cables on the edge.

Shaping the neckline (over 20 rows): the moss stitch is extended over 10 more stitches. The outside edge maintains the mock cable stitch edge. (Follow Chart 6 or the written instructions.)

Next rows:

Row 1, 3, 5: (P, k) 7 times, k20, p2, k2, p2.

Row 2: P2, k2, p2, k20, (p, k) 7 times.

Row 4: P2, LTW, p2, k20, (p, k) 7 times.

Neckline opening

Row 6: P2, k2, k2, k20, (p, k) 2 times, BO10. (30 stitches remain on loom).

Row 7: Join yarn by peg 12. (p, k) 2 times, k20, p2, k2, p2.

Row 8: P2, LTW, p2, k20, (p, k) 2 times.

Row 9: (P, k) 2 times, k20, p2, k2, p2.

Row 10: P2, k2, p2, k20, (p, k) 2 times.

Row 11: (P, k) 2 times, k20, p2, k2, p2.

Row 12: P2, LTW, p2, k20, (p, k) 2 times.

Chart 3: Left Side Panel

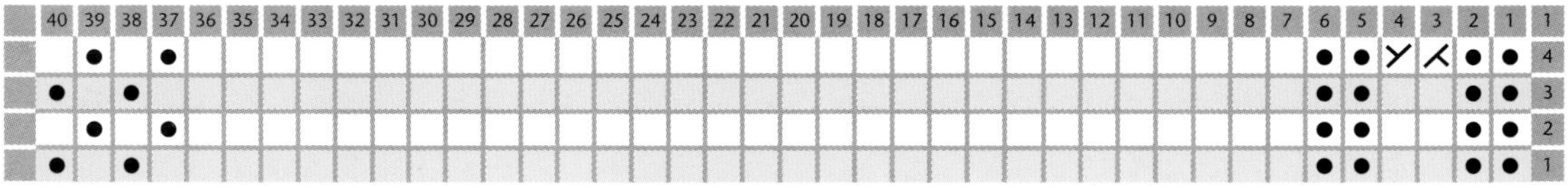

Legend:

knit

purl

Right Twist

Notes: Left Side Panel

Chart 4: Right Side Panel

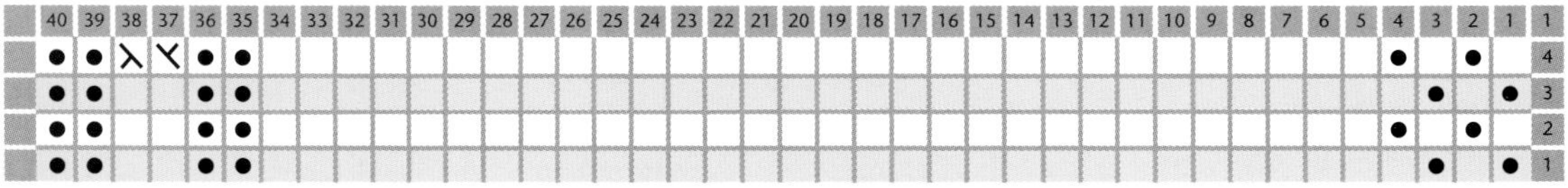

Legend:

knit

purl

Left Twist

Notes: Beginning of Right Side Panel

Chart 5: Left Side Neckline Shaping

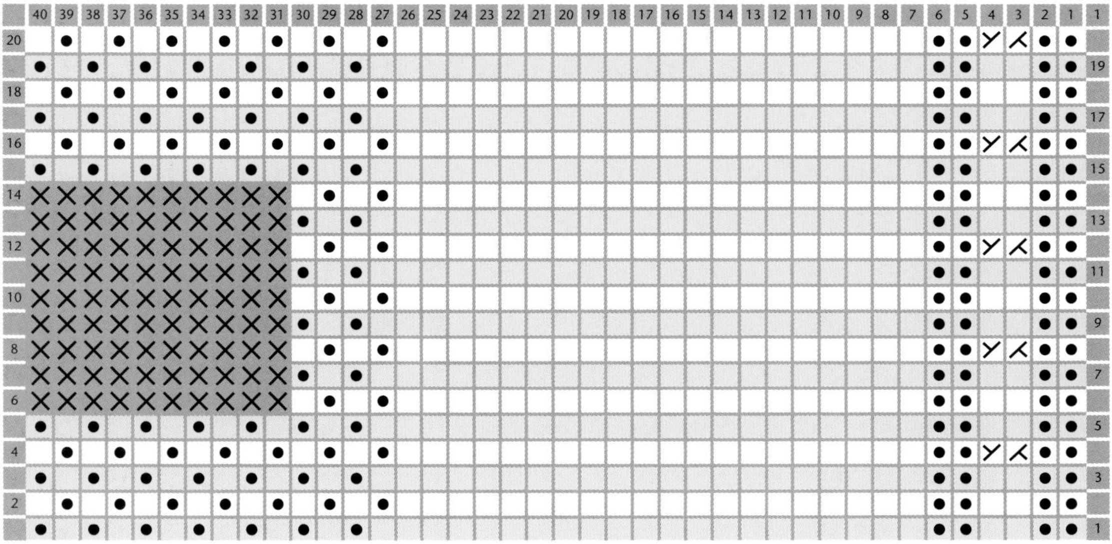

Legend:

knit

purl

Right Twist

No Stitch

Row 13: (P, k) 2 times, k20, p2, k2, p2.
Row 14: P2, k2, p2, k20, (p, k) 2 times.
Row 15: CO10, (p1, k1) 2 times, k20, p2, k2, p2 (40 stitches total).
Row 16: P2, LTW, p2, k20, (p, k) 7 times.
Row 17: (P, k) 7 times, k20, p2, k2, p2.
Row 18: P2, k2, p2, k20, (p, k) 7 times.
Row 19: (P, k) 7 times, k20, p2, k2, p2.
Row 20: P2, LTW, p2, k20, (p, k) 7 times.
End of Neckline shaping.

**Next row: K34, p2, k2, p2,
Next row: P2, k2, p2, k34
Next row: K34, p2, k2, p2
Next row: P2, LTW, p2, k34**
Rep from ** to ** 24 more times (you should have 25 mock cables).
Knit 6 rows of Moss Stitch.
Bind off with basic removal method. Block panels lightly.

Part III Assembly

Place both panels right side up on a flat surface. Arrange the panels so they are mirror images of each other. The neckline opening should be a rectangle in the center. The mock cables should be on the outside edge, while the moss stitch edge should be at the middle of the front side; the back side should have the stockinette edge against each other.

Seam the back side of the ruana with a mattress stitch seam.

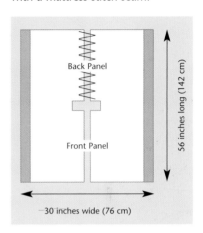

Chart 6: Right Side Neckline Shaping

Legend:

☐ knit

● purl

⅄ ⅃ Left Twist

✕ No Stitch

Notes: Right Side Panel: Neckline shaping chart

Waves Shrug

When you do not want to wear a sweater, or a shawl, the shrug comes to the rescue. A mix of a short shawl and a bolero, the Waves Shrug will keep your arms and back warm. The Waves Shrug is knitted with a simple purl and knit design that will remind you of small waves hitting the shore.

You will need

Knitting Loom

Knitting Loom with at least 60 pegs [Regular Gauge Hat Loom by Décor Accents was used in sample]

Yarn

400 yds. (366 cm) of bulky weight yarn. [Berroco Softwist, 59% rayon, 41% wool, 100 yds (92 m) per 1.75 oz (50 g) used in sample]

Notions

Knitting tool
Tapestry needle

Size

44 ins. x 17 ins.
(112 cm x 43 cm)

Gauge

16 sts and 24 rows to 4 ins. (10 cm) in stockinette stitch

Pattern notes

Knit as a flat panel
K = knit = knit stitch/flat stitch
M1 = Make 1 (creates an increase)
K2Tog = Knit 2 stitches together (creates a decrease)

Stitch Patterns
• Rib Stitch Pattern
Multiple of 4
Row 1: *K2, p2; rep from * to end.
Row 2: *P2, k2; rep from * to end.

Legend:
☐ knit
● purl

Wave Stitch Pattern
Multiple of 12
Row 1: P2, k7, p3
Row 2: K2, p2, k5, p2, k1
Row 3: K2, p2, k3, p2, k3
Row 4: K4, p5, k3
Row 5: Knit
Row 6: Knit

Legend:
☐ knit
● purl

Note: Item is knitted all in one flat panel. Knit extra/fewer stitch pattern repeats in the body of the shrug to make the shrug longer or shorter.

Cuff

Cast on 52 stitches with crochet chain method

Row 1: *K2, p2; rep from * to end.
Row 2: *P2, k2; rep from * to end**
Repeat from ** to ** until cuff measures 8 ins. (20.5 cm) from cast-on edge. End on a row 2.
Next row: K2, m1, k1, p2, *k2, p2; rep from * to last 2 sts, m1, p2 (54 sts).
Next row: P3, *k2, p2; rep from * to last 3 sts, k3.
Next row: K2, m1, k2, p2, *k2, p2; rep from * to last 5 sts; k2, p1, m1, p3 (56 sts).
Next row: P4, *k2, p2; rep from * to the last 4 sts; k4.
Next row: K2, m1, k3, p2, *k2, p2; rep from * to last 2 sts, m1, p3 (58 sts).
Next row: P5, *k2, p2; rep from * to last 5 sts; k5.
Next row: K2, m1, k4, p2, *k2, p2; rep from * to last 3 sts; p1, m1, p3 (60 sts).
Next row: Knit.

Body

Knitted in Wave Stitch Pattern.

Row 1: *P2, k7, p3; rep from * to end.

Row 2: *K2, p2, k5, p2, k1; rep from * to end.

Row 3: *K2, p2, k3, p2, k3; rep from * to end.

Row 4: *K4, p5, k3; rep from * to end.

Row 5: Knit.

Row 6: Knit**

Repeat from ** to ** until body area measures 28 ins. (72 cm) ending with a row 6.

Cuff

Next row: K2, k2tog, k2, p2, *k2, p2; rep from * to last 4 sts; p2, p2tog, p2 (58 sts).

Next row: P5, *k2, p2; rep from * to last 5 sts, k5.

Next row: K2, k2tog, k1, p2, *k2, p2; rep from * to last 7 sts, k2, p1, p2tog, p2 (56 sts).

Next row: P4, *k2, p2; rep from * to last 4 sts, k4.

Next row: K2, k2tog, p2, *k2, p2; rep from * to last 6 sts; k2, p2tog, p2 (54 sts).

Next row: P3, *k2, p2; rep from * to last 3 sts, k3.

Next row: k1, k2tog, p2, *k2, p2; rep from * to last 5 sts, k2, p2tog, p1 (52 sts).

Next row: *P2, k2; rep from * to end.

Next row: *k2, p2; rep from * to end**.

Repeat from ** to ** until ribbing measures 8 ins. (20.5 cm).
Block lightly. Bind off.

Assembly

Fold piece lengthwise. Mattress stitch seam the cuff area plus 4 ins. (10 cm) or until you reach the desired place.

PART II
Board Knitting

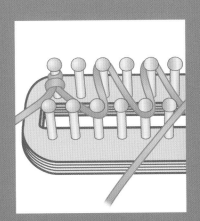

Knitting Boards

Get ready to create in double knit. Here you will learn the process of using a knitting board to create beautiful double-sided items that use both sides of the loom.

A knitting board is a frame that has two rows of pegs facing each other. The knitted garment passes through the center of the frame and comes out the bottom of the frame. In order to create a double-sided item, you will weave yarn from one side of the board to the other side. A knitting board is also known as a double-sided rake. Consequently, a knitting board can also be used as a knitting rake—by using only one side.

Knitting Board Gauges and Yarns

The gauge of the board is determined by the distance from center of peg to center of peg as well as by the distance between the two rows of pegs. The gauge of the board will determine the type of yarn you can use on it. The desired look of the knitted garment will determine what type of board and yarn you would need to use.

Currently there is no standard uniform knitting board gauge terminology amongst loom manufacturers, and one vendor's regular gauge may be equivalent to another vendor's large gauge. The following are general guidelines on the yarn types to use on the different knitting boards available.

Large Gauge
1 strand of bulky weight yarn or 2 strands of 4 ply worsted weight.

Regular Gauge
1 strand of 4 ply worsted weight yarn.

Small Gauge
1 strand of 4 ply worsted weight yarn.

Fine Gauge
1 strand of 4 ply worsted weight or fingering weight yarn.

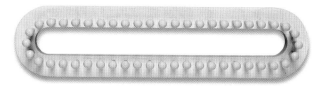

GLOSSARY

Circular The result of wrapping all the pegs on the board is called a circular. To complete a circular with Stockinette Stitch and Rib Stitch—you wrap the board from left to right, then from right to left.

The Knitting Board

Some notes before we embark on our Double Knit adventure:

- A knitting board has two rows of pegs facing each other. For demonstration purposes, we will name one side, side A, the opposite side, side B.
- The pegs will be numbered as 1A, 1B, 2A, 2B—each pair of pegs is known as a set.
- Work on the board from left to right.

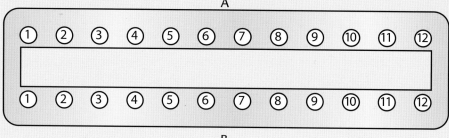

Basic Cast on

1

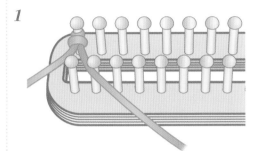

Make a slip knot and place it on the first top peg of the knitting board (peg 1A).

2

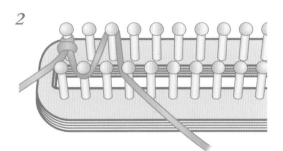

Take working yarn down to peg 2B, wrap around it. Go up to peg 3A, wrap around it, then down to peg 4B, wrap around it. Continue in this manner, skipping every other peg, until you reach the end of the board (or the number of stitches you want to cover for your pattern).

3

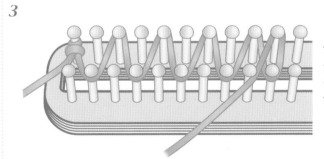

To complete the circular go to the peg directly across, wrap it. Continue wrapping the pegs that were skipped in Step 1.

Anchor Yarn

Place a piece of contrasting yarn in the middle of the board. The yarn is called an anchor yarn and needs to be long enough to thread the ends down through the center gap of the board and tie them together, thus securing the cast-on row of stitches.

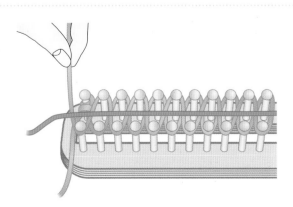

The anchor yarn has two purposes.
1 It aids in pulling your item down the center of the board.
2 It helps you identify the live stitches that you will be binding off later.

Knitting Board Stitches

Once your cast-on row is finished you are ready to begin knitting with the desired pattern stitch. Take you pick from the ones below.

Basic stockinette

Basic stockinette is achieved by wrapping the board in the same manner as the cast on row on the previous page.

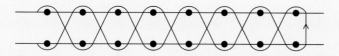

Start at peg 1A. Take working yarn down to peg 2B, wrap around it. Go up to peg 3A, wrap around it, then down to peg 4B, wrap around it. Continue in this manner, skipping every other peg, until you reach the end of the board (or the number of stitches you want to cover for your pattern). To complete the circular go to the peg directly across, wrap it. Continue wrapping the pegs that were skipped in Step 1. **Knit Over process:** Start by knitting the first 2 sets of pegs at each end of the board, then knit the middle pegs.

The Stockinette Stitch produces a very tight weave

Rib stitch

Woven on the board and similar to the stockinette cast on, except rib is worked at a slight angle. Note: you must cast on with an even number of pegs.

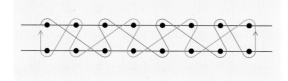

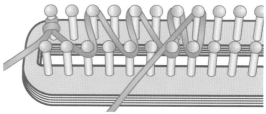

Start at 1A, down to peg 3B, up to peg 3A, down to peg 5B, then up to 5A. Continue weaving your yarn, skipping every other peg. You will be wrapping at a slight angle. When you reach the end of the board wrap the upper and lower pegs directly across from each other. Turn your board around and cover all the pegs that you skipped to complete a circular. **Knit Over process:** First knit the first 2 sets of pegs at each end of the board, then knit the middle pegs. Repeat.

Rib Stitch has the rib look on both sides. Like regular needle ribbing, the ribbing on the board can be used for cuffs where you would want a snugger fit.

Simple Stitch

Simple stitch provides an open weave, perfect for thick yarns. Also known as the zigzag stitch, and the fashion stitch, in the simple stitch, a circular is completed in one pass down the board.

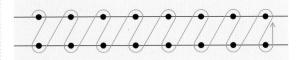

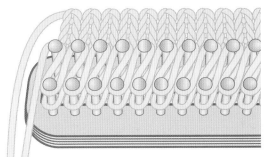

Start at top 1A peg, down to bottom 1B peg, then up to top 2A peg, then down to bottom 2B peg. Continue down the board covering all the pegs. The yarn will be towards the outside of the peg.

Knit over process: knit over all down one side; then knit over the opposite side. Anchor the yarn first by knitting over the last peg wrapped first.

Note: Always start knitting over on the same side.

Next row: Wrap the opposite peg, continue wrapping down the board. Be sure to wrap the pegs in the same direction as the previous row. Note: The first peg is not wrapped—it becomes a turning peg.

Knit over process: Knit over all down one side; then knit over the other side. Knit over on the last peg wrapped first to anchor the yarn. **Note:** Always start knitting over on the same side. Repeat.

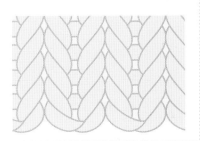

Figure 8 Stitch

The figure 8 stitch is a very open airy stitch, perfect to use with novelty yarns and super bulky yarns. It allows the yarns to "fluff" and look their best.

The Figure 8 stitch is also used to cast on extra stitches at the beginning or end of the board.

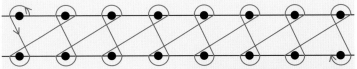

Start at top peg 1A, go around it, towards the outside of the loom. Take it down to peg 1B with yarn between peg 1B and peg 2B, wrap around the peg, then go up to peg 2A, between peg 2A and peg 3A, wrap around peg 2A, then go down to peg 2B. Continue to the end of the board. Repeat the same weaving for the next rows.

Knitting Over process: knit over on one side of the board, then knit over on the opposite side. Always start knitting over on the same side.

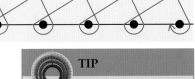

TIP

Place a stitch marker or a contrasting piece of yarn on the side that you need to knit over first.

Practice Project

Power Pink Scarf

Hip scarf knitted with a fun novelty yarn. It is a quick knit on a large gauge knitting board. Knit it longer than necessary for a fashionable look.

You will need

Knitting Loom

Large gauge knitting board [Pink Knifty Knitter board was used in sample]

Yarn

140 yds. (128 m) of bulky weight novelty yarn [3 skeins of Patons Twister 65% Polyester, 35% Acrylic, 47 yds. (43 m) to 50 g was used in sample]

Tools

Knitting tool
Tapestry needle

Size

Size: 68 ins. x 4 ins.
(173 x 10 cm)

Gauge

Not important

Pattern notes

Knitted completely with figure 8 stitch. The figure 8 stitch allows for an open weave stitch that permits the "feathery" properties of the Twister yarn to fluff up.

Instructions

Cast on 8 sets of stitches (16 pegs total: 8 from each side).

Row 1: Knit with the figure 8 stitch.

Next rows: Repeat Row 1 until scarf reaches desired length.

Bind off loosely. Weave in ends.

Color changes

Designing with stripes is easy and it could provide you with an original item.
Gather all your odd skeins and sit down and loom knit a one-of-a-kind item.

Creating horizontal stripes is the easiest way to give your knits a fresh look. Always change yarns at the beginning of a row. To attach the new color/skein, leave a 5–8 ins. (12.5–20 cm) beginning tail.

Insert the beginning tail of the new yarn through one of the stitches in the center of the board. Lay the two ends in the center—the ends will be hidden between the knitting.

Wrap with the new color/skein down the board in the established pattern.

will run from peg to peg. Knit over as usual. Continue wrapping in the established pattern.

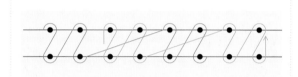

Checkerboard Pattern

To change the colors around to create a checkerboard pattern, change the wrapping process: wrap the pegs that were wrapped with MC with CC, and vice versa.

Vertical stripes

These are created by using the simple stitch or the figure 8 stitch. Locate the area where you want the stripes to begin. Insert the beginning tail end through one of the stitches in the center of the board. Lay the tail end in the center of the board; once you start weaving and knitting, the tail end will be hidden.

Since you will be dealing with two strands of yarn within the same row, you need to do the wrapping in two steps. Pick up the main color yarn (MC) and wrap all the pegs desired in that color. Be sure to wrap it in sets (1A, 1B, 2A, 2B, and so on). At the end of the row, drop the MC. Go back to the beginning of the row, pick up the contrasting color (CC) and wrap the pegs skipped. The unused color

Shaping

Increasing and decreasing on a knitting board is similar to shaping in the round. Two methods will be demonstrated below. Make sure you have only 1 loop on each peg to start.

Increasing Method 1

Method 1—recommended use when casting on more than 2 stitches.

Inc1: To increase the number of stitches, simply Figure-8 wrap the next set of empty pegs twice. Wrap the other pegs so that the entire board has 2 loops on each peg. Knit over as usual.

This type of increase method leaves a step edge. For a gradual increase, try the next method.

For example, the knitting board below has stitches from pegs 2–7. Increase at peg 8 by Figure-8 wrapping peg 8A and 8B twice. Increase on the other side by Figure-8 wrapping peg 1A and 1B twice.

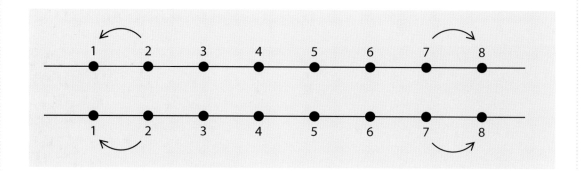

Increasing Method 2

Make 1—recommended use when increasing only 2 stitches at a time.

The make 1 (m1) increase method is completed within a row. It provides a gradual increase that leaves a clean angled edge.

Move the last set of stitches outwards to the next set of empty pegs. You have created an empty set of pegs. With your knitting tool or crochet hook, reach in and pick the running strand from one peg to the next, twist it and place it on one of the empty pegs. Reach for the strand on the other side, twist it and place it on the other empty peg. Wrap your board as usual; all pegs should have 2 loops on them. Knit over as usual.

For example, assume you have stitches from pegs 2–7. Move the stitches from pegs 7A and 7B to the empty pegs 8A and 8B. You have created an empty set of pegs and increased by 1 stitch. Reach for the ladder going to peg 6A, twist it and place it on empty peg 7A. Reach for the ladder going to peg 8B, twist it and place it on empty peg 7B.

You can also create an empty set of pegs other than at the end of the board. Just move all the stitches one space over, leaving an empty space where you want the increase to happen.

To create a less noticeable increase—increase every 3–4 rows.

Decreasing Method 1

Use this at the very end/beginning of a row.

Dec: The decrease is similar to the increase method with the exception that the stitches need to move towards the center of the board. The pegs adjacent to the decrease will have an extra stitch.

1 Move the last stitches inwards to the adjacent peg.
2 Wrap and knit over. Make sure to knit over 2 over 1 on the pegs with the extra stitches.

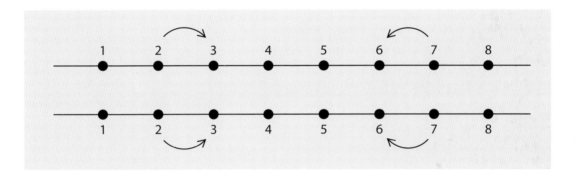

Decreasing Method 2

Use this within the row: It creates a more gradual decrease.

Let's assume you have all the pegs covered as in the diagram above. You want to decrease by 2 stitches at each end.

K2tog: Move the stitches from pegs 7A and 7B to pegs 6A and 6B. Move the stitches from pegs 8A and 8B to pegs 7A and 7B—one decrease done on the right side of the loom. Wrap the board as called for in the pattern and knit over as usual. When you reach the pegs with 3 loops on them, knit over the bottommost 2 stitches. Pegs 8A and 8B are empty.

I recommend Method 2 for most decreases as it leaves a less noticeable decrease angle. To make it more subtle—increase every 3–4 rows.

Finishing Techniques

Binding off and finishing your work on a board loom is similar to working in the round.

A few more techniques become possible.

Binding Off on a Board

Prepare: Locate a crochet hook that works with the yarn for the project. Each peg must have only 1 loop.

Cut working yarn leaving a 6 inch (15 cm) tail. Begin on the opposite side where the yarn tail is located.

1

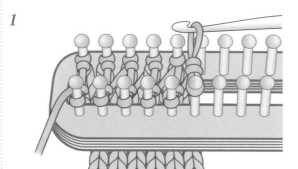

With crochet hook, remove loop from peg 1B, leave it on the crochet hook. Remove loop from top peg 1A, place it on crochet hook. Remove loop from top peg 2A, place it on the hook. The crochet hook should have 3 loops on it.

2

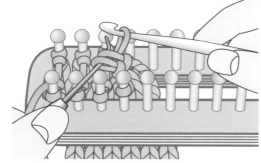

Slip two stitches through the back loop on the hook. One stitch remains on the crochet hook.

3

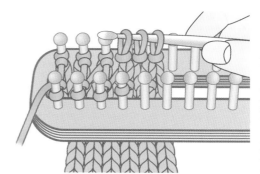

Remove the loop from peg 2A, place it on crochet hook. Remove loop from top peg 3B, place it on crochet hook. Crochet hook has 3 loops again. Slip the 2 stitches through the back stitch. One stitch remains on crochet hook.

4

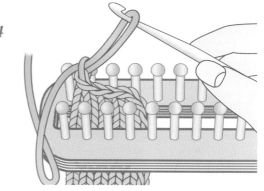

Repeat until you reach the end of the board and all the stitches have been removed. Catch the tail end and hook through the last loop on the crochet hook. Tighten and weave in the ends.

Finishing Off the Cast-On Edge

The anchor yarn is holding the first loops as "live" stitches. When the project is completed, the cast-on edge needs to be finished by crocheting. The following steps will show how to accomplish this essential step of the knitted garment. In order to finish the "live" stitches, you need to have a crochet hook that will work with the weight of yarn used.

1

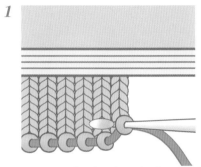

Insert crochet hook in the first stitch.

2

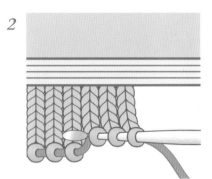

Insert the hook through the next two stitches.

3

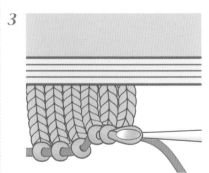

Pass the first stitch on the front of the hook through the middle stitch, and then pass it through the back stitch, leaving only 1 loop on the hook.   .

4

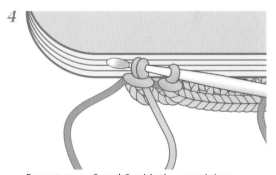

Repeat steps 2 and 3 with the remaining stitches. When you reach the end, form a chain with the yarn tail end and pass it through the last loop. After all the stitches have been bound off with the crochet hook, you can remove the anchor yarn by pulling it out.

Practice Project

You will need

Knitting Loom

Knitting board with at least 12 sets of pegs
[Pink Knifty Knitter was used in sample]

Yarn

65 yds. (60 m) of bulky weight yarn
[Berroco Pleasure, 66% Angora, 29% Merino Wool, 5% Nylon, 130 yds (119 m) per 50 g was used in sample]

Tools

Knitting tool
Crochet hook
Decorative pin

Size

17 ins x 4 ins.
(43 cm x 10 cm)

Gauge

11 sts and 14 rows =
4 ins. (10 cm)

Scarflet

A small project to learn decrease/increase on a knitting board. Use a special brooch to give this small scarflet a unique touch.

Pattern notes

Knit completely in stockinette stitch.
K2tog = knit 2 together, creates a decrease. (Move the stitches inwards, then weave and knit).

Instructions

Cast on 12 set of stitches.
Knit for 14 ins. (36 cm) in stockinette stitch.

Decrease row: K1, k2tog, knit to last 3 sts, k2tog, k1.

Next two rows: Knit**.
Repeat from ** to ** 3 times (6 sets of sts will remain on knitting board).
Bind off.

Board Patterns

Knitting on a straight board creates a much thicker knitted fabric than regular circular loom knitting. This is where the quality of loom knitting really comes into its own.

Double Knit Ribbed Scarf

Alpaca yarn is perfect for this project—soft and cozy to keep you extra warm during the winter months. The ribbed structure of the scarf allows it to sit comfortably around the neck.

You will need

Knitting Loom

Knitting board with at least 12 sets of pegs
[Pink Knifty Knitter was used in sample]

Yarn

220 yds. of super bulky weight yarn
[Misti Alpaca Chunky 108 yds. (99 m), 100 g per hank used in sample]

Notions

Knitting tool
Crochet hook

Size

76 x 5 ins.
(193 x 12.5 cm)

Gauge

11 sts and 14 rows to
4 ins. (10 cm)

Pattern notes

Knit in Rib Stitch throughout

Instructions

Cast on 12 stitches.
Knit for 76 ins. (193 cm) in rib stitch. Bind off. Block lightly.

Striped Scarf

Don't hide your true stripes. Use odds and ends of yarn that you have in your stash already to get creative. Experiment by varying the width of the stripes, or even make the stripes in a novelty yarn for extra fun.

You will need

Knitting Loom

Knitting board with at least 12 sets of pegs.
[Pink Knifty knitter was used in sample]

Yarn

125 yds. (114 m) MC, 50 yds. (46 m) CC of super bulky weight yarn [Caron Simply Soft Quick, 100% acrylic, 50 yards (46 m) per 3 oz. skein, was used in sample]

Tools

Knitting tool
Crochet hook

Size

72 ins. x 5 ins.
(183 cm x 12.5 cm)

Gauge

10 sts and 12 rows
to 4 ins. (10 cm)

TIP

When doing small stripes (1–3 rows) it is not necessary to cut the yarn. Carry the colors up the side weaving in at the end of each row.

Pattern notes

Knit completely in Stockinette Stitch

Instructions

Cast on 12 sets of pegs with MC.
Knit 6 rows with MC. Join CC. Knit 2 rows with CC. Cut CC, leave a 5 ins. (12.5 cm) tail. Repeat from ** to ** until scarf measures 70 ins. (178 cm) from cast-on edge. Knit 6 rows with MC. Bind off.

PART III
Felting

Loom Knitting Felts

A decade or so ago, I acquired a gorgeous cashmere sweater. It was my favorite sweater to wear. Then, the dreaded day came when I had to wash it.

Although I read the instructions on the label, my inexperience won and I threw it in the laundry with all my other clothes. Then, the most devastating moment occurred—my sweater was big enough to fit a newborn baby. I quickly assumed that it was the washer that had caused the shrinkage in my lovely sweater. Fast forward a few years and now I am throwing things in the washer to make them smaller on purpose.

Since the death of that sweater, I have learned that it was not the washer that killed it, but a combination of different factors. The agitation in the washer, the changes in water temperature, and the detergent all combined to open the scales of the fiber, and as the scales opened, they interlocked with each other forming a thick, impermeable fabric. The sturdy fabric created by felting (also known as "fulling") is perfect for many items like bags and slippers.

Yarns for Felting

In order to felt successfully, the item needs to be knitted loosely with non-super-wash wool, or yarns that have a high natural fiber content like mohair, llama, angora, or alpaca.

Light color yarns such as white and off-white take longer to felt than dark colored yarns and at times, they do not felt. The reason for light colored yarns felting at a slower rate is because they have been through a bleaching process that has damaged the scales. Before felting with any light colored yarns, make sure to knit a test sample swatch.

The easiest way to find out the properties of the yarn is its label. Common telltales that the yarn may felt: Wash by hand with cold water. Fiber content. If the yarn is labeled Supewash—stop, do not start your project with it. Superwash yarn has been treated to be machine washable and its felting capabilities have been treated.

Items to be felted need to be knitted at a very loose gauge; for this reason, the large or extra large gauge knitting looms are preferred.

You are probably ready to cast on your knitting loom—but let's wait for a bit. Although we will be purposely shrinking our knitted fabric, making a swatch can tell us many things about our yarn. Certain yarns tend to felt very quickly, while others may take up to four cycles, yet others may not even show any tendency to felt at all.

Quick Yarn Felting Test

Cut about 2 yards (2 m) of yarn. Fill a small bowl with warm water and a drop of dishwashing soap. Immerse the yarn and roll it around your palms; keep rolling it for about 5 minutes. Take it out and inspect it—pull at it. If the yarn has clumped together and does not come apart, then the yarn has felting capabilities.

Felting Swatches

Before embarking on your felting adventure,
you need to make a swatch—no really, you do.

These will allow you to see how the yarn behaves. Knit a small sample. I prefer to knit a square about 10 ins. x 10 ins. (25 cm x 25 cm), a sample size that can always be used as a coaster or as a pocket inside a bag.

Knit your swatch using the same yarn and stitch you plan to use for your project. If using color combinations, knit the sample with the same color combinations. Some yarns, even same brand yarns, do not felt at the same rate. Be sure to knit your sample swatch with the exact yarn you are planning to use with your project. Before throwing it in the washer, let's mark it up to learn how much shrinkage to expect. Use cotton thread in a contrasting color (don't use the same color as you may not able to see it after it is felted) to mark 4 inches (10 cm) of stitches, and 4 inches (10 cm) of rows. Felt your sample swatch and allow it to air dry. Measure your

felted gauge by finding the thread markers and measuring. If you have gauge, you may go forth and begin your project. If gauge was not achieved, try with a different yarn.

Let's Shrink It

It has been said that felting knitted items is an art more than a science. You come by it by inspiration. Each felted item is unique. Enjoy the adventure!

What you need

These are the main items you will need apart from your yarn and loom.

Zippered Pillowcase

This splendid item will allow the knitted item to be kept separate in the washer. It keeps all the fiber away from the washer's drain. Using the zippered pillowcase protects the knitted item from distorting inside the washer as it prevents it from becoming tangled.

Agitator Helpers

Take a trip to the local thrift store and pick up a pair of light colored jeans for light felted knits and a pair of dark colored jeans for dark knits. Try not to use towels as agitator helpers as they may shed lint on your felted item and you'll end up with unwanted speckles.

Soap

No-rinse wool soap or shampoo will allow the scales of the wool fibers to soften during the wash. I like to use Eucalan Wool Wash as it has a hint of lavender and it subdues the wet, woolly smell.

Felting it

1 Place the knitted item inside the zippered pillowcase. Close the zipper.

2 Set the washer to the smallest size setting and hottest wash.

3 Add a teaspoon of shampoo or no-rinse wool wash. Throw in the agitator helpers, throw in the zippered pillow case. Close the door and start the washer.

4 Check the process after five minutes. Stop the washer. Reach in and take out the zippered pillowcase. If the item is the desired size, take it out. If the item is not the desired size, throw it back in the zippered pillowcase and re-start the washer. Check again in a few minutes. Do not let the washer go into the spin cycle. The spin cycle can create creases in your project.

5 When item has reached the desired size. Remove it from zippered pillowcase and rinse it out (if you used shampoo). Rinse it in the same water temperature as in the washer. If you used no-rinse wool wash you do not need to rinse.

6 Place item between two towels and squeeze out as much water as possible.

Pull it into Shape

Your item is felted, your masterpiece is almost done; all it needs is a place to take its destined shape. If possible, find a suitable shape for your masterpiece to mold itself on. Find a box for bags or make one out of two pieces of cardboard and use plastic bags to cover them and to use as filler for the inside. Other items like slippers can be filled with plastic bags for the toe and a piece of cardboard for the sole (cover the cardboard with plastic bags). Go ahead and pull and tug your felted item into shape. If one of the corners is not looking the way you imagined, pull it into shape.

Allow your felted item to air dry completely; you can take the shape helpers out after 12 hours to speed up the drying process inside the item. Do not put the felted item in the dryer as this can shrink your item further.

Troubleshooting

How do I know when it is ready?

Look closely at your fabric; do you like the look of it? Some loom knitters like their knitted items to have stitch definition. If you like the way it looks, it is ready. If the item is not the desired size, then it is not ready.

It is too big

If your item is too big, throw it back in the washer for a few more minutes/cycles. Keep a close watch and keep washing it until it reaches the desired size.

It is too small

Do not despair, everything is not lost. Wet the item completely and try to pull it to the desired dimensions. If after pulling and tugging the desired sized is not achieved, try looking for the silver lining. Cut the felted item into other usable items: coasters, eyeglasses case, small coin bag, or even a small bedroom rug.

It is out of shape

No, it doesn't need to go on the treadmill; it is not that kind of out of shape. If the item is crooked, try stretching it into the desired shape, pin it down and allow it to air dry pinned down.

Caring for your Felted Knits

You can handwash soiled felted knits in warm water. Do not over-rub them; simply immerse them in the water and gently wash.

Fuzzy problems: If the item has become extra fuzzy, use a razor to trim out all the excess fuzz.
Stretch problems: Handles are particularly prone to become elongated with prolonged use. Sew a piece of grosgrain ribbon to the underside. Use the same type of ribbon to stabilize bag openings.

Practice Project

Yoga Mat Bag

Learn the basics of felting with this easy yet useful project. Choose a fun yarn to create a unique-to-you bag. Don't do Yoga? It's okay, knit it anyway and use to store your expanding long knitting loom collection.

You will need

Knitting Loom

Large gauge circular knitting loom with 36 pegs [Green Knifty Knitter was used in sample]

Yarn

300 yards (274 m) of bulky weight wool [Manos del Uruguay, 100% wool, 137 yards (125 m) per 100 g was used in sample]

Tools

Knitting tool
Tapestry needle

Other

Yoga Mat for blocking purposes

Size

24 ins. x 6 ins.
(61 cm x 15 cm)
circumference (felted dimensions)
32 ins. x 8.5 ins.
(81 cm x 21.5 cm)
circumference (non-felted)

Gauge

8 sts and 10 rows to
4 ins. (10 cm)

Pattern notes

K = Knit = Knit Stitch/Flat Stitch
P = Purl

Stitch Pattern

Garter Stitch (gs)
Round 1: Purl **Round 2:** Knit

Instructions for Bag

Cast on in the round with cable cast on method.

Knit in garter stitch until item reaches 32 ins. (81 cm) from cast on edge. Bind off with gathering removal method.

Strap

Knitted as flat panel.
Cast on 12 sts with cable cast on method.

Knit in garter stitch until item reaches 36 ins. (91 cm) from cast on edge. Remove using basic removal method.

Assembly

Attach strap to open rim (secure tightly). Attach strap to the bottom of the bag, place it about 3 inches (8 cm) away from the center of gathering removal. Felt as per felting instructions. To block, insert yoga mat inside and allow to air dry.

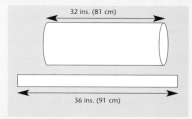

Felting Patterns

When the yarn mats together it creates a much stronger and denser fabric that is less prone to stretching. This means felting is ideally suited to things that get a lot of wear, like bags and slippers.

Felted Accessories Clutch

A small purse to carry all your essential loomy tools. This small clutch takes only a small amount of yarn and, knitted on a large gauge knitting loom, can be knitted in a jiffy.

You will need

Knitting Loom

Large gauge knitting loom with a minimum of 26 pegs
[Yellow Knifty Knitter was used in sample]

Yarn

55 yds. of bulky weight yarn [Lion Brand Landscapes, 50% wool/ 50% Acrylic, 55 yards (50 m) per 1.75 oz. (50 g) used in sample]

Other

10 ins. (25.5 cm) zipper

Tools

Knitting tool
Tapestry needle

Size

Pre-felted: 11 ins. x 10.5 ins. (28 cm x 26.5 cm)
Felted: 9 ins. x 10 ins. (23 cm x 25.5 cm)

Gauge

9.5 sts and 16 rows to 4 ins (10 cm)

Pattern notes
Knitted as a flat panel
Knit = Knit Stitch/Flat Stitch

Garter Stitch:
Row 1: Purl.
Row 2: Knit.
Rep above two rows.

Instructions
Cast on 26 stitches with chain cast on method.

Row 1: Purl.
Row 2: Knit.

Rep above 2 rows, until panel measures 10.5 ins. (26.5 cm) from cast on edge.

Bind off with basic bind off method.

Assembly
Fold in half and seam along the two sides. Felt as per felting instructions. When dry, attach zipper to opening.

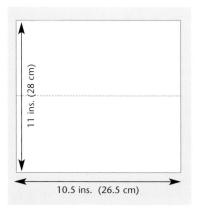

11 ins. (28 cm)

10.5 ins. (26.5 cm)

Felted Handbag

With its subtle gray and green stripes, this felted tote is perfect for everyday use, and will complement most outfits. Lilac and blue stripes also work well. The bag is completed on a round, large gauge knitting loom with at least 50 pegs, which is ideal for projects of this size.

You will need

Knitting Loom

Any large gauge loom with at least 50 pegs, for example, the blue Knifty Knitter Long Loom

Yarn

250 yds. (229 m) bulky weight wool in color A, 125 yds. (114 m) bulky weight wool in color B, 125 yds. (114 m) bulky weight wool in color C

Tools

Knitting tool
Darning needle
Spool

Size

14 ins. x 10.5 ins. (36 x 27 cm)

Gauge

Pre-felted: 12 sts and 16 rows to 4 ins. (10 cm)

Pattern notes

Knitted completely in garter stitch. One garter stitch repeat = Row 1: Knit, Row 2: Purl.

Tote Side 1

With color A, cast on 50 stitches with cable cast-on method.
Rows 1–16: Knit 8 garter stitch repeats. Cut color A, leaving a 6-ins. (15-cm) yarn tail. Attach color B.
Rows 17–26: Knit 5 garter stitch repeats. Cut color B, leaving a 6-ins. (15-cm) tail. Attach color C.
Rows 27–30: Knit 2 garter stitch repeats. Cut color C, leaving a 6-ins. (15-cm) tail. Attach color B.
Rows 31–32: Knit 1 garter stitch repeat. Cut color B, leaving a 6-ins. (15-cm) tail. Attach color C.
Rows 33–36: Knit 2 garter stitch repeats. Cut color C, leaving a 6-ins. (15-cm) tail. Attach color B.
Rows 37–46: Knit 5 garter stitch repeats. Cut color B, leaving a 6-ins. (15-cm) tail. Attach color A.
Rows 47–62: Knit 8 garter stitch repeats. Bind off 8 stitches each side (leaves 34 stitches on the loom).

Tote Base (34 stitches)

Rows 1–32: Knit 16 garter stitch repeats.

Tote Side 2

Cast on 8 stitches on each side (total 50 stitches).
Rows 1–16: Knit 8 garter stitch repeats. Cut color A, leaving a 6-ins.

(15-cm) yarn tail. Attach color B.
Rows 17–26: Knit 5 garter stitch repeats. Cut color B, leaving a 6-ins. (15-cm) tail. Attach color C.
Rows 27–30: Knit 2 garter stitch repeats. Cut color C, leaving a 6-ins. (15-cm) tail. Attach color B.
Rows 31–32: Knit 1 garter stitch repeat. Cut color B, leaving a 6-ins. (15-cm) tail. Attach color C.
Rows 33–36: Knit 2 garter stitch repeats. Cut color C, leaving a 6-ins. (15-cm) tail. Attach color B.
Rows 37–46: Knit 5 garter stitch repeats. Cut color B, leaving a 6-ins. (15-cm) tail. Attach color A.
Rows 47–62: Knit 8 garter stitch repeats.
Bind off completely.

Handles

Using the spool, make two, 3-peg I-cords, 20 ins. (51 cm) long.

Assembly

Seam the tote panels at the sides to form the tote. Felt (see page 126). Attach the handles. Hold the two sides of the tote together and, with a darning needle, poke a hole through both panels, about 2 ins. (5 cm) from the top edges and 6 ins. (15 cm) from one seam. Pass the needle through both holes. Repeat 6 ins. (5 cm) from the other seam. Pass one I-cord through the two holes on one panel, and form a knot at each end inside the tote. Repeat on the other panel.

Felted Laptop Cozy

Finally a way to keep your laptop scratch-free with this super-easy bag. The felted properties make it ideal for a laptop cozy as it will help keep moisture away in case of an accident. Show your school/sassy spirit by knitting the cozy in school colors!

You will need

Knitting Loom

Large gauge knitting loom with at least 41 pegs
[Yellow Knifty Knitter was used in sample]

Yarn

320 yds. (293 m) of super bulky weight wool [Rowan Big Wool, 100% wool, 87 yards (80 m) per 100g, was used in sample]

Tools

Tapestry Needle
Knitting tool

Gauge

Pre-felted: 12 sts and 16 rows to 4 ins. (10 cm)

Size

Pre-felted:
16 ins x 16 ins.
(41 cm x 41 cm)
Felted:
13 ins x 13 ins. x 2 ins.
(33 cm x 33 cm x 5 cm)

Pattern notes

K = knit = knit stitch/flat stitch
P = purl
Sl = slip stitch
BO = bind off
CO = cast on
Stockinette stitch = knit every row
MC = main color
CC = contrasting Color
Knitted as a flat panel.

Instructions

Note: Slip the first stitch on every row.

Cast on 41 sts with MC.
Knit 3.5 ins. (9 cm).

Next row: Sl1, k13, BO13, k14.
Next row: Sl1, k13, CO13 with e-wrap method, k14.

Knit in stockinette stitch for 10 ins. (25.5 cm). Cut MC. Join CC.

Knit in stockinette stitch for 2 ins. (5 cm).

Next row: P
Next row: K
Next row: P

Knit in stockinette stitch for 2 ins. (5 cm). Cut CC. Join MC.

Knit in stockinette stitch for 10 ins. (25.5 cm).

Next row: Sl1, k13, BO13, k14.
Next row: Sl1, k13, CO13, k14.

Knit in stockinette stitch for 3.5 ins. (9 cm).
Bind off all stitches with basic removal method.

Fold in half. Seam the sides. Felt as per felting instructions.

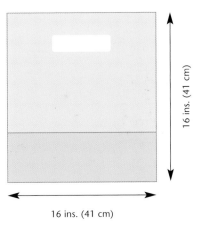

16 ins. (41 cm)

16 ins. (41 cm)

Soft Felt Slippers

I remember my feet dangling down from the chair with a pair of big red comfy slippers that my Grandma had knitted for me. The slippers in this pattern are a slide-on style—a quick knit and a perfect last-minute gift.

You will need

Knitting Loom

Large gauge round knitting loom with at least 31 pegs [Red Knifty Knitter was used in sample]

Yarn

120 yds. (110 m) of bulky weight non-superwash wool [Brown Sheep Lamb's Pride Bulky, 85% Wool, 15% Mohair, 125 yds, (114 m) was used in sample]

Tools

Tapestry Needle
Knitting tool
Stitch markers

Gauge

8 sts and 10 rows to 4 ins. (10 cm)

Size

Women's sizes 6 (7, 8)

Pattern notes

Knitted as flat panel and in round. W&T=wrap and turn. Lift the loop off the peg, hold it with tool. E-wrap peg, replace loop back on peg. Turn and knit in the other direction.
KO 2/1= knit the bottom 2 loops over and off the peg.
Important: Add suede bottoms to make them slip-resistant.

Instructions

Make 2. Place stitch marker on pegs 1 and 16. Cast on 16 stitches and proceed to make the heel as follows:

**Row 1: K from peg 1–15; W&T peg 16.
Row 2: K from peg 15–2; W&T peg 1.
Row 3: K from peg 2–14; W&T 15.
Row 4: K from peg 14–3; W&T 2.
Row 5: K from peg 3–13; W&T 14.
Row 6: K from peg 13–4; W&T 3.
Row 7: K from peg 4–12; W&T 13.
Row 8: K from peg 12–5; W&T 4.
Row 9: K from peg 5–11; W&T 12.
Row 10: K from peg 11–6; W&T 5.
Row 11: K from peg 6–12; KO 2/1 on peg 12.
Row 12: K from peg 12–5; KO 2/1 on peg 5.
Row 13: K from peg 5–13; KO 2/1 on peg 13.
Row 14: K from peg 13–4; KO 2/1 on peg 4.
Row 15: K from peg 4–14; KO 2/1 on peg 14.
Row 16: K from peg 14–3; KO 2/1 on peg 3.
Row 17: K from peg 3–15; KO 2/1 on peg 15.
Row 18: K from peg 15–2; KO 2/1 on peg 2.
Row 19: K from peg 2–16; KO 2/1 on peg 16.
Row 20: K from peg 16–1; KO 2/1 on peg 1.**
Knit 18 (20, 22) rows in stockinette stitch.

Next row: K16, CO 15 with e-wrap method (31 sts on loom). Begin knitting in the round. Knit 14 (16, 18) rounds.

Toe

Next rows: Knit from ** to **. Remove stitches from the knitting loom onto two knitting needles: Place sts 1–16 on one needle. Place sts 17–31 on second needle. Seam the toe with Kitchener stitch.

Top bumper instructions:

Make 2. Cast on 3 sts. Knit a 15 (16, 17) inch (38, 41, 43 cm) length I-cord.

Assembly

Attach I-cord to top of slipper: start right below the instep area of the slipper and continue towards the heel and ending on the other side. Felt as per felting instructions (see page 126). Add suede soles.

Useful Information

Reading Charts

Charts are pictorial representations of stitch patterns, color patterns, or shaping patterns.

Reading charts in loom knitting differs from reading a chart when needle knitting. In needle knitting, the knitting is turned after every row, exposing the wrong and right side of the fabric every other row. In loom knitting, the right side of the fabric is always in front, so we follow the pictorial chart as it appears.

- Charts are visual and pictorial representations of the stitch pattern. A chart allows you to see the entire stitch pattern.
- Charts are numbered on both sides, even numbers on the right side, odd on the left.
- Start reading the chart from the bottom.
- Each square represents a stitch.
- Each horizontal row of squares represents a row.
- Stitch pattern charts use symbols to represent stitches such as knit, purl, twists, yarn-overs, and any other stitch manipulation needed.
- Thick black lines represent the end of a pattern stitch repeat. The stitches after the black line are edge, or selvedge, stitches.
- Charts for color knitting differ from stitch pattern charts. In color pattern charts each different color square represents the color needed for that particular stitch.

- For Circular Knitting: read the chart from bottom up from right to left.
- For Flat Knitting: read the chart from bottom up from right to left on odd rows, and from left to right on even rows.
- Remember: the right side of the knitted fabric is always facing the outside. Knit the stitches as they appear on the chart.

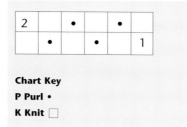

Chart Key
P Purl •
K Knit □

Chart reads:

For Flat Knitting:
Row 1: k1, p1, k1, p1.
Row 2: k1, p1, k1, p1.

For Circular Knitting:
Round 1: *k1, p1, rep from * to the end.
Round 2: *p1, k1, rep from * to the end.

A complete list of chart symbols and abbreviations used in this book is provided on the opposite page (we are using needle knitting standard abbreviations and symbols whenever possible).

Washing your knits

Hand washing is the best washing technique for all your knitted items. Even those items that were knitted with machine washable yarns can have their life extended by practicing good washing habits.

Use a pure soap flakes or special wool soap. Wash and rinse your item gently in warm water. Maintain an even water temperature; changing water temperature can shock your wool items and accidentally felt them. Before washing, test for colorfastness. If the yarn bleeds, wash the item in cold water. If the yarn is colorfast, wash with warm water.

Fill a basin or sink with water, add the soap flakes or wool soap, using your hands, gently wash the knitted item. Avoid rubbing, unless you want the yarn to mat and felt together.

To rinse, empty the basin and fill with clean warm water, immerse your knitted item and gently squeeze out all the soapsuds. Repeat until all the suds are gone and the water is soap free. Pat as much of the water out as you can use the palms of your hands. Do not wring your item as this may cause wrinkles and distort the yarn. Place the knitted item between two towels and squeeze as much of the water out as you can.

To dry your item, lay it flat away from direct sunlight. Block again, if necessary, to measurements.

Head Size Chart for Hats

Once you have got the hang of making hats you will want to design your own, or convert the patterns here to your own ends. Use this chart as a guide only to the average head sizes to help you.

	Size	Circumference	Depth
Preemie	Preemie 1–2 lbs (0.45–0.9 kg)	9–10 ins. (23–25.5 cm)	3.5–4 ins. (9–10 cm)
	Preemie 2–3 lbs (0.9–1.4 kg)	10–11 ins. (25.5–28 cm)	4 ins. (10 cm)
	Preemie 4–5 lbs (1.8–2.3 kg)	11–12 ins. (28–30 cm)	4 ins. (10 cm)
	Preemie 5–6 lbs (2.3–2.7 kg)	12–13 ins. (30–33 cm)	5 ins. (12.5 cm)
Baby	Newborn	13–14 ins. (33–36 cm)	5–6 ins. (12.5–15 cm)
	Baby 3–6 months	14–16 ins. (36–41 cm)	6–7 ins. (15–18 cm)
	Baby 6–12 months	16–19 ins. (41–48 cm)	7 ins. (18 cm)
Children	Toddler	18–20 ins. (46–51 cm)	8 ins. (20.5 cm)
	Child	19–20 ins. (48–51 cm)	8 ins. (20.5 cm)
Young Adults	Teens	20–22 ins. (51–56 cm)	9–10 ins. (23–25.5 cm)
Adults	Adult Woman	21–23 ins. (53–58 cm)	10 ins. (25.5 cm)
	Adult Man	22–24 ins. (56–61 cm)	10 ins. (25.5 cm)

Hats need to be loom knitted with a 1 inch (2.5 cm) negative ease for a close fit, that is the hat should be slightly smaller when measured flat than the head it is to fit.

Poncho Conversion Chart

The lovely poncho pattern that we have supplied is designed for a small child. However, you can use the pattern provided here and adapt it to your own measurements. Use the table below to find the exact size of panels you need to make for your desired poncho size; then you can make one for every member of the family.

	Size	Panel Size Length	Panel Size Width
Baby/Toddler Size	12 Mos	13 ins. (33 cm)	6.5 ins. (16.5 cm)
	2 Yrs	19 ins. (48 cm)	9.5 ins. (24 cm)
	4 Yrs	21 ins. (53 cm)	10.5 ins. (27 cm)
Child Sizes	6 Yrs	22 ins. (56 cm)	11 ins. (28 cm)
	8 Yrs	23 ins. (58 cm)	11.5 ins. (29 cm)
	10 Yrs	25 ins. (64 cm)	12.5 ins. (32 cm)
	12 Yrs	27 ins. (69 cm)	13.5 ins. (34 cm)
	14 Yrs	28 ins. (71 cm)	14 ins. (36 cm)
	16 Yrs	29 ins. (74 cm)	14.5 ins. (37 cm)
Woman's Size	x-small	28 ins. (71 cm)	14 ins. (36 cm)
	Small	29 ins. (74 cm)	14.5 ins. (37 cm)
	Medium	31 ins. (79 cm)	15.5 ins. (39 cm)
	Large	31.5 ins. (80 cm)	15.75 ins. (40 cm)
	1X	32 ins. (81 cm)	16 ins. (41 cm)
	2X	33 ins. (84 cm)	16.5 ins. (42 cm)
	3X–4X	34 ins. (86 cm)	17 ins. (43 cm)
	5X	34.5 ins. (88 cm)	17.25 ins. (44 cm)

Common Abbreviations Found in Loom Knitting

[ ]	work instructions in brackets as many times as directed
( )	work instructions in parentheses in the place directed
* *	repeat instructions between the asterisks as directed
*	repeat instructions following the single asterisk as directed
alt	alternate
approx	approximately
beg	begin/beginning
bet or btw	between
BO	bind off
but	buttonhole
CA	color a
CAB	cable
CB	color b
cbs	chunky braid stitch
CC	contrasting color
ch	chain (use a crochet hook)
cm	centimeters
cn	cable needle
co	cast on
col	color
cont	continue
cr l	cross left
cr r	cross right
dbl	double
dec	decrease
diam	diameter
ds	double stitch
ew	e-wrap
foll	follow/following
fc	front cross

fs	flat stitch/knit stitch
g	denotes grams
g st	garter stitch
hs	half stitch
inc	increase
K or k	knit
kbl	knit through back of loop. In looming this is created by e-wrap
k2tog	knit 2 together—creates a right slanting decrease.
l	left
lc	left cross
lp(s)	loop (s)
LTW	left twist
m	denotes meters
M1	make one. increase one stitch
MC	main color
mm	denotes millimeters
mul	multiple
oz	denotes ounces
P or p	purl
p2tog	purl 2 stitches together—a right slanting decrease
pm	place marker
prev	previous
psso	pass slipped stitch over
rc	right cross
rem	remaining/remain
rep	repeat
rev St st	reverse stockinette stitch
rnd(s)	round(s)
RS	right side
RTW	right twist
sc	single crochet
sel	selvedge
sk	skip
skn	skein

skp	slip, knit, pass stitch over—creates a decrease
sl	slip
sl st	slip stitch
ss	single stitch
ssk	slip, slip, knit these two stitches together—creates a left slanting decrease
ssp	slip, slip, purl these two stitches together—creates a left slanting decrease
st(s)	stitch(es)
St st	stockinette stitch (knit every row)
tog	together
tw	twist stitches for a mock cable
W&T	wrap and turn
yds.	yards
yo	yarn over
zip	zipper

Resources

Knitting Looms

The knitting looms used in this book were provided by two vendors, Décor Accents, Inc., and Provo Craft. If you would like to find a larger variety, do an internet search for knitting looms or loom knitting and you will find a larger selection at your fingertips.

Décor Accents, Inc.
PO Box 541
Newton, UT 84332
www.dalooms.com
info@dalooms.com

Provo Craft
151 East 3450 North
Spanish Fork, Utah
84660
www.provocraft.com

Yarns

Berroco, Inc.
14 Elmdale Rd.
PO Box 367
Uxbridge, MA 01569
info@berroco.com
www.berroco.com

Brown Sheep Yarn Company
10062 County Road 16
Mitchell, NE 69357

Crystal Palace Yarns
160 23rd St
Richmond, CA 94804
www.straw.com

Joann.com
2361 Rosecrans Ave
El Segundo, CA 90245

Knitting Fever, Inc.
PO Box 502
Roosevelt, NY 11575
www.knittingfever.com

Koigu Wool Designs
RR #1
Williamsford, ON N0H 2V0
Canada
info@koigu.com

Lion Brand Yarns
135 Kero Road
Carlstadt, NJ 07072
www.lionbrand.com

Manos del Uruguay
www.rosiesyarncellar.com

Misti Alpaca
PO Box 2532
Glen Ellyn, Illinois, 60138
www.mistialpaca.com

Muench Yarns
285 Bel Marin Keys Blvd
Unit J
Novata, CA 94949
www.muenchyarns.com

Patons
PO Box 40
Listowel, ON N4W 3H3
Canada
www.patonsyarns.com

Plymouth Yarn Co.
PO Box 28
Bristol, PA 19007
pyc@plymouthyarn.com
www.plymouthyarn.com

Westminster Fibers
4 Townsend West
Nashua, NH 03063
www.rowan.com

Dedication

To my favorite people in the world: my husband Samuel and children, Bryant and Nyah. Thank you for your love, patience, and encouragement in my loom knitting endeavors.

Publisher's Acknowledgments

Thank you to Paul Forrester for photography, and the patient models: Jenny Doubt, Chris Lockwood, Bara Plevova, and Victoria Wiggins, plus Matilda Doran Jumaili, Alyssa Deacon, Ethan Deacon, Lois Durows, Lucy Grant, and Connor O'Neil. Thanks also to parents Maz Al-Jumaili, Nicola Deacon, Lisa Durows, and Jane Laing.

Index

Bold page numbers denote projects.

Author's Acknowledgments

Thanks go first to all my friends in the loom knitting community—I would not have been able to write this book without your encouragement, input and support. Our love for loom knitting has given birth to this book.

Loom on!

Special Thanks to:
My editors Katy Bevan and Ruth Patrick for their encouragement, keen eye and creative advice. Anthony Duke, for the most outstanding artwork ever seen in loom knitting.

My loom knitting friends and cheerleaders: Tina Edgar, for encouraging me to write the book and supporting me through the process in more ways than I can ever say; Becky Hansen, for her encouragement and technical support; Lori Lemiux, for introducing me to the world of felting; and to my non-loomy friends: Miriam Felton and Kimberly Petersen, for believing in me and cheering me on. A gigantic warm thanks to Yarn Today in Smithfield, UT, for providing some of the yarns used in this book, especially to Rita Ehrhart for helping me choose the most appropriate yarns for the projects—purple hugs and kisses, my friend.